a CORNER BOY *Remembers*

· GROWING UP IN ST. JOHN'S ·

FRANK J. KENNEDY

BREAKWATER BOOKS LTD.
100 Water Street • P.O. Box 2188
St. John's • NL • A1C 6E6
www.breakwaterbooks.com

Library and Archives Canada Cataloguing in Publication

Kennedy, Frank J., 1921-
    A corner boy remembers / Frank J. Kennedy.

ISBN 1-55081-062-6

1. Kennedy, Frank J., 1921-. 2. St. John's (N.L.)--History--Anecdotes.
3. St. John's (N.L.)--Biography. I. Title.

FC2196.26.K45A3 2006   971.8'103092   C2006-903984-4

© 2006 Frank J. Kennedy
Editor: Jocelyne Thomas

The Canada Council | Le Conseil des Arts
for the Arts | du Canada

We acknowledge the financial support of
The Canada Council for the Arts for our publishing activities.

We acknowledge the support of the Government of Newfoundland and Labrador,
Department of Tourism, Culture and Recreation for our publishing activities.

 We acknowledge the financial support of the Government of
Canada through the Book Publishing Industry Development
Program (BPIDP) for our publishing activities.

Printed in Canada.

DEDICATION

This book is dedicated to my wife, Ruth,
to honour our Golden Wedding Anniversary.

To our daughter, Florence,
for her support and encouragement.

To Glen Power for solving unexpected problems that
sometimes cropped up with the computer.

To my grandson, Geoffrey, for transferring the nearly
50,000 words to a CD for the publisher.

I want to express my sincere thanks to my cousin,
John Kennedy Jr., for his research and for obtaining with
some difficulty, many of the old photos used in the book.

Thanks also to Len Madden for his reminiscences of
our school days and to my cousin Dr. Paul O'Neill for
refreshing my memory of certain events noted here.

I'm very grateful to my distant American cousin,
Joanne Connors, in Miami, Florida,
for her research into the Kennedy genealogy.

Special thanks to Mr. Clyde Rose of Breakwater
and Mr. Wade Foote, General Manager, for undertaking
the publishing of this book. Also Rhonda Molloy and
Kim O'Keefe for their invaluable help.

Thank you to all!

CONTENTS

chapter 1

HOME
DELIVERIES

· NEW BABIES CAME IN SATCHELS ·

Being actually born in a house at the corner of Patrick and Pleasant Streets and living there for three decades must certainly put me in the classification of "Corner Boy", but not, hopefully, fitting Webster's definition as "Street rough, loafer". One thing that I do remember in particular when growing up in the 1920s and '30s was the abundance of home deliveries of various goods and services available. We had no supermarkets, and of course, what you've never had you don't miss. We really didn't need these super stores. Groceries were delivered by the family grocer and there were dozens of these in the city. I remember my mother calling Tom Malone's on New Gower Street once or twice a week and the groceries she ordered would be delivered that same day.

Every morning a man we knew as Mr. Lester from Mount Pearl delivered fresh milk right to our door. An empty quart bottle was placed on the doorstep at night and in the morning he replaced it with a full bottle. He was paid monthly. The milk in those days was not homogenized, which meant the cream would rise to the top of the bottle. We, as kids, loved that and when mom was not around we would take a mouthful right from the bottle. That was a real treat. Not only did Mr. Lester deliver milk to the door every day, but every Christmas he also gave us a free Christmas tree.

A lot of molasses was consumed back then. Everyone had 'lassie' cookies and many people used molasses in their tea instead of sugar. That sweetener, however, was one of the few items that were not delivered. In order to get this product you had to take a container to the store where the molasses was kept in a large wooden barrel, called a tierce (about ninety gallons), with a tap on one end. We had a special crockery jar and would buy a pint at a time from Andrew Duffy's store just across from our house on Patrick Street. One day my mother sent my older brother, Eugene, over to the store for a pint but he forgot to take the jar. When Mr. Duffy asked him what he would put the molasses in, Eugene replied, "Put it in a paper bag." Nevertheless, Eugene turned out to be a smart fellow and always came first in his class in school.

Every Saturday a farmer came to our door selling fresh country eggs from his big round basket covered with straw. Eggs in the grocery stores were imported from the mainland by firms such as Clancy & Co. and George Neal Ltd., but many residents would gladly pay a higher price for the fresh product. In the late '30s, however, when I went to work as an office boy with Clancy & Co., I began to wonder about the quality of those "fresh country eggs" sold door to door by that farmer. At Clancy's I noticed a familiar-looking man arriving every Saturday by horse and cart and buying thirty dozen eggs, which he would put into a big round basket and cover with straw. The same man returned about two hours later for another thirty dozen and often made three or four trips each

Saturday. So much for fresh country eggs! However, when I see eggs in a supermarket today with a "best before" date about a month away, I think maybe those eggs were not so bad after all.

Fresh bread was delivered daily to the grocery stores by the four local bakeries: Walsh's, McGuire's, Central and Mammy's. I remember seeing the bread wagon stopping at Duffy's frequently. The driver would open two doors at the rear of the wagon and use a broom handle with a nail in it to reach in and pluck out the loaves and put them into a huge basket. The bread was never wrapped.

Very few homes had fridges in the 1930s but some had ice-boxes and a block of ice was delivered to homes as required. In our area a Mr. Hickey came around with his horse and a wagon filled with large blocks of ice. Right there on the street he broke off big chunks and brought them into the homes with a strange-looking tool resembling a giant pair of tongs. Many children followed the ice wagon, grabbing chips of ice that fell off as Mr. Hickey chopped away at the big slabs. To us, sucking on these small pieces of ice on a hot summer day, as we held them in a piece of newspaper, was better than ice cream. Well, cheaper anyway. For those who had no iceboxes, fresh meat was delivered daily by butcher shops scattered throughout the city. I remember my mother phoning Mr. Squires on Hamilton Street every morning except Sunday, and ordering stewing meat, frying meat, sausages or whatever she wanted for that day, and the delivery was made within a couple of hours. On Saturdays a 'meat man' came in from the country with his covered wagon. On the back of this were two doors similar to the bread wagon's and when opened, exposed various cuts of meat and a set of hanging scales. This is how we usually bought our Sunday roast. That butcher had asked my mother to save all her potato peelings and each week he gratefully collected them to feed his pigs. Other weekly deliveries included scalded fresh cream in jam crocks and fresh butter. It was all very tasty but what struck me as peculiar was that the "fresh" butter was always very salty. In the fall you could buy blueberries, bakeapples, strawberries and other berries at the door, as well as fresh rabbits and sometimes even partridge. Other good sellers were bundles of splits or kindling for starting coal fires, and birch junks. Every house had a coal stove in the kitchen and coal was delivered by the ton. Ours was dumped near a basement window. We hated that as my brothers and I had to shovel the coal in through the window, which was three feet above ground level. And that was the soft coal. The hard coal for the furnace had to be

A typical small grocery store in St. John's in the 1920s and '30s. There was at least one on nearly every street before the large supermarkets took over the food business. There were four within three minutes walk of this writer's home on the corner of Patrick and Pleasant Streets.

carried in, in buckets, and put into an inner coal pound. We envied people living on New Gower Street. They had coal chutes, the tops of which were level with the sidewalk. Not much hard work there!

Once a week a Chinese gentleman called at our house with a big blue bag on his back and collected our soiled laundry. That was before electric washing machines were common. He would put a special mark on the various items with an indelible pencil. I still remember our mark as "31P." It didn't mean much to us but I'm sure to him it meant, "Mrs. Kennedy, 142 Patrick Street." In a few days he returned with everything nicely washed, ironed and folded. Great service.

Family doctors made "deliveries" to homes as well back then. My mother told me doctors brought babies in satchels to sick women. It happened one day when a doctor visited Mrs. Crotty, who with her husband, Pat, had rented some rooms in our house. I hadn't noticed that Mrs. Crotty had been putting on weight lately and after the doctor was in her bedroom for about an hour, I heard a baby crying. I asked my mom what was going on and she told me the doctor had just brought a new baby to Mrs. Crotty. I said I didn't think so, as I saw the doctor arriving and he had no baby with him. My mother asked if I had seen the large satchel he was carrying. When I said I did, she told me that's where the baby was. Before I got around to asking her where *he* got the baby, she ordered, "Run out and play now Frank. That's the good boy."

chapter 2

THE EARTHQUAKE
AND TIDAL WAVE OF 1929

· AN UNDERGROUND RUMBLE
AND THE HOUSE BEGAN TO SHAKE ·

I remember the earthquake and tidal wave of 1929. Thirty-six people lost their lives on the Burin Peninsula and property damage amounted to more than two million dollars. I had just arrived home from school on that gray November Monday, the 18th. We had recently made a bedroom on the ground floor of our home for my father, who had developed what was then known as "creeping paralysis", and was confined to bed. My mother and I sat talking with him when suddenly we heard an underground rumble and as the sound increased, the house began to shake. We thought it might be a large truck passing by on the street but when we looked out the window there was no traffic to be seen. On the hearth in front of the fireplace were two large seashells, conchs, which my father had brought back from South America. They started to rattle on the porcelain tiles. There must have been a loose clapboard on back of the house for I recall the sound of slap, slap, slap, as it kept hitting the moving building. As the house continued shaking and the rumble grew louder, my father sent me out to the kitchen to look at our hot water boiler. I ran out and looked at it, ran back and told him it was okay. Then he told me to go down in the basement and look at the furnace. The house was still shaking as I started down the stairs and so was I by now. I was only eight years old and was afraid to go down more than a couple of steps, so after a slight pause, I came back and reported the furnace was okay too. By that time the noise and shaking had stopped. My father said, "I believe that was an earthquake."

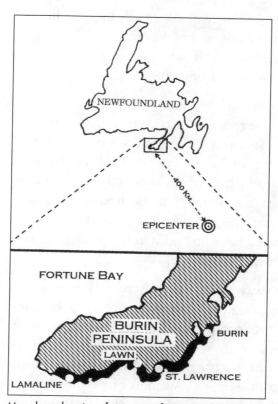

Map shows location of epicenter of 1939 earthquake. Heavy black line in enlarged section indicates area of the Burin Peninsula that was devastated by the tidal wave.
Map by Frank Kennedy

It was indeed an earthquake, the worst ever recorded in Newfoundland, and the epicenter was 250 miles southeast of the Burin Peninsula. It registered seven on the Richter scale. Scientists believe a huge section of the ocean floor collapsed under the weight of the ocean. When this happened and the sea in the area dropped, the water in some areas drained away and the levels dropped a frightening thirty feet, exposing the bottoms of some harbours and leaving scores of fishing boats aground. Some residents who witnessed the phenomena, fearing the water would rush back, ran to higher ground and thereby saved their lives. And rush back it did, in the form of a giant tidal wave eighty kilometers long and as high as a three-story building. It washed away houses, wharves, stages, boats and barns, and unfortunately dozens of people.

Incredibly, news of the disaster did not reach St. John's for three days. There were no road or telephone connections with the Burin Peninsula and the only means of communication was by Morse code sent by the telegraph offices by wire. Dozens of telegraph poles had been knocked down and washed away and the area was literally cut off from the outside world until a coastal boat, the S.S. Portia, called in on its routine visit to St. Lawrence. That ship had wireless apparatus and the shocked crew sent word to St. John's.

Worst hit was Lamaline, where ten people died. Seventy kilometers along the coast in Burin, ten people lost their lives. Fourteen residents in smaller settlements were killed by the wave. Many of these people were inside their homes when the wave came ashore. Some houses were destroyed on the spot while others were washed out to sea and in some cases families that were still inside the floating buildings were rescued by neighbors in small boats. In Ship Cove a family was horrified to feel their home being swept out to sea. As they looked out the windows a second wave struck and pushed the house back onto land and they were all unharmed.

Nearly 500 houses and other buildings were destroyed as well as two dozen schooners and 100 fishing boats. When word of the disaster reached St. John's, the *S.S. Meagle* was sent to the area with doctors and nurses to tend to the many people who had been injured. A special Disaster Committee was formed and a quarter of a million dollars was raised to aid the survivors in the forty towns and fishing villages that were involved in the tragedy.

Schooner lies at anchor awaiting high tide when it will tow house back to shore in St. Lawrence.
Photo courtesy of "The Rooms" Provincial Archives Division

chapter 3

THE
MOVIES

The movies were a great form of entertainment for young and old alike in the 1920s and '30s before television came to Newfoundland. Especially popular were the Saturday matinees, which were attended by thousands of children in St. John's. When I was first taken to the movies at the age of six by my older brothers, silent pictures were still in vogue; they were not the jumpy speeded-up pictures we sometimes see to-day when an old silent clip is shown on TV. We went early to get a seat. We knew we'd get in to the theater but if you were late you'd have to stand up for the full two-hour show. There were no safety regulations in place as there are today and the aisles were often filled with kids standing there enjoying the show. Occasionally an aroma would waft through the air indicating that some little child sitting there knew he could never make it to the washroom through the crowded aisles and could hold it no longer. Admission to the show was five cents.

Westerns, or "cowboy pictures" as they were called, were all the rage and we loved them. Although the pictures were silent, the theater was far from that. There was always a piano near the screen with a pianist playing appropriate music during the show. When the posse was chasing the bad guys, and this happened frequently, the tempo would be stepped up to suit the action on the screen, but often the stamping of feet and the shouting of encouragement to the riders would drown out the sound of the piano. At the Queen Theater the pianist was Miss Mary Power and when she arrived before the show and marched up the center aisle with her sheet music in hand she got a round of applause from the waiting children. By far the most popular man in St. John's was Mr. Charlie Roud, manager of the Queen, which had 1400 seats and was the largest movie house in Newfoundland. The building had four huge windows on one side with two open shutters on each. (See photo on page 18.) When Mr. Roud appeared at the front of the theater there was another round of applause and as he proceeded to close the first shutter, loud cheering erupted, repeating each time a shutter was closed. Just before the last window was blacked out, the house lights came on to another round of cheers, and finally when Mr. Roud walked proudly up the center aisle to open the curtains on the stage, he received the most enthusiastic ovation of all. And then, on with the show.

Our heroes were Buck Jones and Tom Mix. The honor of being the world's first Cowboy Movie Star belongs to Bronco Billy (Anderson). He appeared in more than 400 pictures, all silent. The dialogue for the silent movies appeared as sub-titles flashed on the screen between scenes, not superimposed as usually happens today. One of my older brothers, Neil or Eugene, would read these for me so that I would know what was going on. By the time I learned to read we had movies

Former Queen Theater in downtown St. John's is destroyed in a spectacular fire. Note the large windows mentioned in the story.
Photo by Frank Kennedy

With 1200 seats, the Paramount Theater on Harvey Road was one of the fine movie theaters in St. John's that closed with the coming of television in the 1950s.
Photo by Frank Kennedy

with sound or "talkies", which arrived in St. John's in 1929. The first sound movie produced was "The Jazz Singer" starring Al Jolson and was made in 1927. It took a while for "talkies" to really catch on because many patrons who were used to talking to one another during the show continued doing that and would miss much of the dialogue. Sometimes the admonishment, "Shut up!" could be heard from annoyed viewers. There were always a few short subjects shown before the main feature: cartoons, newsreels, travelogues, etc., and occasionally some of these would be silent. I remember my sister Eileen coming home from a movie one day and saying there was a cute, "Felix the Cat" cartoon shown. I asked her if it was a "talkie" and before she could answer, my other sister Mary interrupted with, "Don't be so foolish Frank, how can a cat talk?" Little did she know of the coming wonders of the silver screen.

Thomas Edison invented the motion picture back in the 1890s, but the term, "motion picture" is a misnomer, as what we see on the screen is a series of still pictures shown at the rate of 24 per second. They blend together and give the illusion of movement. Edison discovered that projecting as few as 16 pictures per second could result in a flicker-free movie, and he asked the Eastman Kodak Company to come up with a celluloid film. For him they made a film 35mm wide with sprocket holes on each side and that's what Edison used for his first movies. It is an amazing fact that more than a hundred years later, this is exactly the same size film with the same size sprocket holes that is used in modern theaters today. The wide screen picture is achieved by using an anamorphic lens on the projector, which stretches the image laterally, giving the wide screen ratio. Of course a similar lens must first be used on the camera to squeeze the image to fit the 35mm frame. The first

The projection room of the old popular Star theater. Small 20-minute film reels are clearly visible under lamp shade at left and at lower right.
Photo by Frank Kennedy

Modern projectors at Studio Twelve are fed by huge rolls of film like this one, shown by manager Bob Antle, and last for an entire two- or three-hour show. The film does not have to be rewound, as it is fed into the projector from the center of the roll.
The Telegram Photo, reprinted with permission

movie shown to an audience was on April 23, 1896, at the Koster & Bials Music Hall in New York city and was shown by Edison himself.

Silent movies taken at the rate of 16 frames per second were shown at the same rate and of course, the motion looked perfectly normal. However, when Warner Brothers added a sound track to one side of the film, it was found that the speed of one foot per second running through the camera was not fast enough to record faithfully the high frequencies and they decided to use 24 frames per second. All modern projectors are set at this speed, and as I mentioned earlier that accounts for the speeded-up motion of old silent films.

In the early days one reel of film would last only 20 minutes but with two projectors the operator could switch over to the second machine when the first reel ran out. With switching back and forth, there was no interruption in the show. Most theaters had two projectionists but the Nickel Theatre had only one and he sometimes fell asleep during the show. When the film ran out, there was a blinding white screen, and after a few seconds, very loud stamping of feet from the irritated audience. This, of course, awakened the operator and the show continued. But he owned the theater and couldn't be fired. Present-day theaters use huge ten thousand-foot rolls of film three feet in diameter and they last for the entire show, so only one projector is required.

Miss Nora Hogan was the first woman to manage a St. John's movie theater. She took over from her brother Ron as manager of the newly opened Capitol Theater in the early 1930s after he passed away. That large auditorium on the third floor of the Total Abstinence and Benefit clubrooms on Duckworth Street was originally known as "The Casino", a high class show place where local performers and many artists from Canada and the United States were well received and were very entertaining. The last theater to open in St. John's before television was the magnificent Paramount on Harvey Road with 1200 plush seats and carpets throughout. It was also managed by Miss Hogan, assisted by Vince Grant. Next door was Frost's Restaurant, which was well patronized by movie goers. With the arrival of television in 1954 people began staying home for entertainment and as attendance dropped off, the nine theaters in the city, the Paramount, the Capital, the York (formerly known at The Queen), the Crescent, the Popular Star, the Majestic, the Cornwall, the Nickel and the Regal (formerly known as the Little Star), gradually closed their doors one final time. With the coming of spectacular special effects and X-rated movies, smaller theaters opened up in the city malls. The Avalon Mall has 12 small theaters each seating from 145 to 345 people.

3-D Movies

Reminiscences of movies in St. John's would not be complete without mention of the 3-D era of the mid-thirties. Three-dimensional movies were absolutely unbelievable. No movie screen today, not wide-screen, not cinemascope, not surround-sound or Cinerama can come close to the realism of that innovation. The principle is quite simple but the application was rather cumbersome. When we look at a scene in real life we are seeing it from two slightly different viewpoints, the distance our eyes are apart − about four inches. With 3-D movies, two cameras were used to take in the same view our individual eyes would see. In the theater, two projectors show the two films simultaneously and with special filters on the projectors and the audience wearing Polaroid glasses, the left eye sees what the left camera "saw" and the right eye what the right camera "saw". The illusion was perfect. In a jungle scene a roaring lion jumped right out of the screen and most of the audience ducked and screamed. A view from inside a fast-moving car looked as if a head-on collision was imminent. People put up their hands to protect themselves from the accident, screaming in terror. In a view from a boat in a stormy sea, people started getting seasick and had to close their eyes. The many different effects were both frightening and very entertaining and realistic. As I stated earlier, the whole process was cumbersome and this is why 3-D didn't last long. For one thing the audience had to wear special Polaroid glasses which were given out on entering the theater. Then special filters had to be used on the projectors and the latter had to be synchronized. Since both machines were used at once, the length of the feature could not exceed about thirty minutes. Normal switching back and forth could not be done. As well, if the filters were accidentally switched on the projectors, the effect was lost. I remember that happening at one showing and after a few minutes looking at a flat picture, I realized what was happening and put the glasses on backwards. The third-dimensional effect was instantaneous. I advised several people seated near me to do the same, which they did and for the rest of the show many people in the audience were staring at us and wondering why we were going mad. 3-D movies turned out to be just a passing fad but it was great while it lasted.

chapter 4

HINDENBURG NEARLY CRASHED in NEWFOUNDLAND

• A FLYING LUXURY LINER •

I remember the day the *Hindenburg* flew over St. John's. It was Saturday July 4, 1936, and there was great excitement that sunny afternoon. I remember also seeing the newsreels of the horrifying crash ten months later. The arrival over the city was unannounced and hundreds of children playing in the streets and their back gardens rushed into their homes telling their mothers to "Come out and see the big balloon!" It was big, certainly, the largest aircraft ever constructed to this day. It was truly a flying luxury liner: 800 feet long and 135 feet in diameter, three and one half times longer than a Jumbo jet; it was the pride of Germany. It came in gracefully and slowly over Signal Hill and flew so low we could see people in the large windows taking pictures. It had flown all the way from Germany and was headed for New York. The four Daimler-Benz engines had been slowed to give the 72 passengers a leisurely look at St. John's. The airship could come to a complete stop in midair if needed and even go in reverse. At full speed the giant zeppelin traveled eighty miles per hour, making a trans–Atlantic crossing in less than three days. This, of course, was long before passenger airplanes flew across the ocean and the usual trip by ocean liner took a week. That summer the *Hindenburg* made ten round trips to the U.S. and seven round trips from Germany to South America, clocking over 200,000 miles and carrying more than 1600 passengers. On two occasions the airship came close to disaster. The first was on its second trip to the States, when it was caught in an unexpected storm over the Atlantic and fell from its normal cruising altitude of 650 feet to within fifty feet of the waves – less than half its diameter. The second near-miss was on the third flight when it flew over Cape Race in a dense fog. For some unknown reason it began losing altitude rapidly until the altimeter indicated it was practically on the ground. Quick action was taken; hundreds of gallons of water ballast were dropped and the ship climbed out of danger.

Passengers on the *Hindenburg* traveled in first class style inside the enormous hull. There were adequate sleeping accommodations in the many private cabins and a first for air travelers, a shower. The dining room boasted white linen tablecloths with sterling silver place settings and bone china dishes. The individual tables were tastefully decorated with a centerpiece of fresh flowers. Food was in abundance and there was a copious supply of fine wines. On a typical Atlantic crossing the chefs would have, for example, 440 lbs. of fresh meat, 65 dozen eggs and 220 lbs. of butter. There were two long promenade decks with huge picture windows and a spacious lounge with a grand piano. One-way fare across the ocean was $400.00, slightly less than a first class ticket on the *Queen Mary*.

When the *Hindenburg* was being built, the intention was to use helium, a non-flammable gas, rather than the highly-flammable hydrogen (then used in other dirigibles) to render them lighter than air. However, helium was produced only in the United States and was forty times more expensive than hydrogen. Not only that, the U.S. had put an embargo on the export of the gas for fear it could be used for purposes of war. The builders were not overly concerned about that as other hydrogen airships had been in service for years without any major problems, particularly the forerunner of the *Hindenburg*, the *Graf Zeppelin*, which was slightly smaller at 775 feet. It had been in service since 1928 and had flown around the world in 1929. In fact they did not even explore the possibility of obtaining helium from the States. A special advantage of using hydrogen was that it was lighter than helium and with it an airship could carry more passengers, more freight and more weight. The hydrogen was contained in sixteen huge bags or cells which took up most of the space inside the aluminum-framed, canvas-covered hull. For safety reasons smoking was permitted only in the smoking room which was slightly pressurized to insure any leaking gas could not enter. Hydrogen is not only colorless but odorless as well. It was felt nevertheless that any slight leakage would cause no great concern, as being the lightest known gas it would rise to the top of the airship and be sucked out through the vents. What's more, all the gas bags were above the living quarters.

In 1937 eighteen round-trip flights were scheduled to the U.S. and although only 36 passengers had boarded for this first trip that was arriving on May 6, the return flight was fully booked. As the airship slowly approached the mooring mast at Lakehurst, New Jersey, at 300 feet the tail dropped slightly as if it was losing gas. Immediately 150 gallons of water ballast were dropped from the stern but this action did not quite bring the ship to an even keel and another 130 gallons were dropped, drenching some of the surprised spectators waiting on the ground. Newspaper photographers, newsreel cameramen and radio news reporters were on hand to cover the season's first arrival. And they got the biggest scoop of their careers. A young announcer from radio station WLS in Chicago, Herb Morrison, was describing the scene and being recorded by his sound technician, Charlie Nehlson. "Here it comes ladies and gentlemen," he began, "and what a sight it is, a thrilling one, just a marvelous sight....The sun is striking the windows of the observation deck on the eastward side and sparkling like glittering jewels against a background of black velvet." Just then a tiny burst of flame appeared on top of the airship near the rear tail fin. In seconds a gigantic orange flash lit up the countryside. Up front inside the control gondola, officers felt a jolt and saw a nearby hanger light up brilliantly. "The ship is on fire!" cried one of the men. As it began to fall, another officer yelled, "Take to the windows!" The blazing stern crashed to the ground at a 45 degree angle and slowly the front came down, allowing many of the passengers and crew to jump out and run for their lives in the few seconds before the airship was completely engulfed in flames. Thirty-five people didn't make it.

Broadcaster Morrison couldn't believe what he was witnessing. He continued, "It's burst into flames! Get this Charlie! Get this Charlie...get out of the way please, oh my, this is terrible...It is burning, bursting into flames and falling on the mooring mast and all the folks we...this is one of the worst catastrophes in the world! Oh! It's four or five hundred feet into the sky. It's a terrible crash ladies and gentlemen...Oh! The humanity and all the passengers." Immediately underneath the *Hindenburg* more than one hundred men, mostly U.S. navy personnel, were standing by to assist in the mooring, When they saw the flaming airship falling towards them they fled the scene, but as the crash came, many rushed back to attempt a rescue and succeeded in assisting many of the injured and getting them away from the flaming wreckage. Sixty-two survived and thirty-six died, including one of the navy men.

An inquiry concluded that as the *Hindenburg* approached the landing field it made a sharp left turn at full speed and this strain on the huge frame probably caused a bracing wire to snap, slicing into one of the rear gas bags. As the hydrogen leaked through the canvas covering it was ignited by static electricity generated by the friction of the hull passing through the air. That disaster marked the end of the great era of airship travel.

The largest aircraft even constructed, the zeppelin *Hindenburg,* flew over St. John's on July 4th,1936. On an earlier flight it nearly crashed at Cape Race.
Re-enactment photo by Frank Kennedy

The DO-X

On May 19th, 1932, four years before the *Hindenburg* flew over St. John's, a huge flying boat landed at Holyrood for a massive fill-up of 7000 gallons of gasoline. It was the German-built DO-X (Dornier-Experimental) seaplane with twelve engines mounted on its 158-foot wing, the largest heavier-than-air craft ever built to that day. When it first flew in 1929, it was realized that although it could carry 170 passengers, it could never be economically feasible to operate. The twelve 525 horsepower engines consumed a vast amount of fuel and although its top speed was over 100 miles per hour, it weighed fifty-five tons and required a crew of thirteen. To the owners' delight and relief, the U.S. Armed Forces agreed to buy the plane if it was delivered in New York. The owners decided to make a goodwill tour of several countries on the way to that city and give demonstration flights and maybe receive an order or two. However, by the time it had visited England, Italy, Africa and South America, and after several breakdowns and waiting months for parts and repairs, it took two years to get to New York. At that late date the Armed Forces' VIPs had changed their minds. Instead, they wanted smaller, faster airplanes. Nevertheless, two orders had been received from Italy and when these planes were delivered they were used as freighters.

With no sale in New York, the decision was taken to keep the plane there over the winter and overhaul the 12 engines, which incidentally had been manufactured in the United States. On May 19th the DO-X took off for a refueling stop in St. John's. The plan was to land in Freshwater Bay and taxi through the Narrows to Imperial Oil's pier at the South side of the harbour. However, after a twelve-hour flight it was discovered that the water in Freshwater Bay was too rough for a safe landing. Holyrood was the second choice but fog there prevented a landing as well. Flying another twenty miles west, the giant aircraft landed safely at Dildo in Trinity Bay, where it remained for the night. Next morning it took off and landed in Holyrood and most of that day was spent refueling. More than one hundred barrels of gasoline were taken by boat and pumped into tanks on the aircraft anchored offshore. Many St. John's residents, who were disappointed at the plane's non-arrival in the city, traveled to Holyrood to see the unusual sight. A special train left St. John's for Holyrood and picked up passengers along the way, returning that same evening. Sightseers came by car, truck, motorcycle and bicycle. It was estimated that more than six thousand people visited the settlement that day.

The huge flying boat, the DO-X, landed in Holyrood in May, 1932 for a massive fill-up of 7000 gallons of gasoline.

Next morning the plane took off for the Azores and finally arrived home to a tumultuous welcome on the twenty-fourth of May. The flying boat was used for some years for sightseeing tours, the cost being subsidized by the Government. In 1936 the DO-X suffered another accident and was taken out of service and ended up in the Luftfahrt Museum in Berlin, keeping company with the Fokker tri-plane of the famous Red Baron. During World War II, allied bombers destroyed the museum and all its contents, putting an absolute end to one of the world's greatest flying boats, exceeded in size a few years later by Howard Hughes' *Spruce Goose*, which flew only once for a few hundred feet and now lies in a museum in New York.

Amelia Earhart

On May 20th, 1929, aviation history was written in Newfoundland. Not only with the presence of the DO-X flying boat in Holyrood, but on that same day Amelia Earhart took off from a small field in Harbour Grace and after 14 hours and 50 minutes, landed on a small farm in Culmore, Ireland, to become the first woman to fly solo across the Atlantic.

chapter 5

TALES
FROM SCHOOL

• FRIGHTENING SOUNDS FROM THE FURNACE ROOM •

My first day at school was very exciting, meeting so many potential friends. My brother, Eugene, who had just graduated from Holy Cross School, brought me down and introduced me to Principal Brother Eagan, a very likable Irishman, who took me to the grade 1 classroom. There was no kindergarten then, we all started in grade 1. Brother G. F. Wakeham, a St. John's man, was in charge and this was his first year teaching, as well. He had his hands full as there were nearly fifty boys in that classroom.

Holy Cross School on Patrick Street was staffed by ten teachers, all Christian Brothers including the principal. Some were Irish, most Newfoundlanders. All the brothers, except one, used the strap occasionally; it was a common form of discipline in the city, but during my ten years at that school, sexual abuse was unheard of. Brother Ryan was the one who used no strap. His method of punishment was amusing. He taught grade 10 and our classroom was in the basement next to the furnace room of the newly constructed monastery.

Infrequently, when a student misbehaved or, in the opinion of the teacher, deserved punishment, Brother Ryan would send him in to the furnace room. Then he would pick up one of his rubber overshoes, march in behind the boy and slam the door. You could hear a pin drop in the classroom as we wondered about the fate of the offender. The silence was shattered by a frightening series of loud slaps after which the door opened and the student emerged with his hair disheveled. It looked as if he'd had a hard time. But actually what happened was when Brother Ryan went into the furnace room he would slap the wall a few times with his overshoe and then with one hand, gently muss up the boy's hair. The boy was warned not to tell anyone what had happened and sent back to his desk. We would never tell our parents we had been punished, thinking they would probably say we deserved it.

Notwithstanding the above, the Brothers in general were a fine group of men and very dedicated teachers. In the early days, before the monastery was built in 1931, all lived at Mount St. Francis Monastery on Merrymeeting Road, two kilometres from the school, and walked back and forth every school day. I don't remember a Brother ever missing a day because of bad weather, even in winter. Brother King (Joey) who taught grade 9, also in the basement, would lock the school door sharp at nine o'clock and anyone who came late was barred out for an hour. At ten o'clock they were let in and kept an extra hour after school. I remember one morning four of us were locked out. There happened to be a wheelbarrow nearby and one of the boys lay down in it and actually fell asleep. The other two boys pushed the wheelbarrow out of the schoolyard, up Patrick Street and down Hamilton Street to the old West End Fire Hall at the corner of New Gower Street and left it there. The passenger didn't even wake up! The three of us were let in at ten o'clock but the other guy never showed up for the rest of the day. Maybe he went home to finish his nap or maybe the firemen discovered him outside their door and gave him a tour of the fire station. At any rate, when he showed up the next morning he mentioned nothing and of course, we did not question him. But he certainly was never late again. Brother King really piled on the homework, especially in winter. In the first three months that year we spent an average of three and a half hours at homework each school day; a total of 170 hours. Small wonder we all passed with flying colors that year.

One day in grade 8, I was not feeling well and my mother kept me home from school that morning. I found out in the afternoon that during the morning session the teacher, Brother O'Dwyer, had left the room for a few minutes and when he returned he found the class in a state of bedlam. He announced that the entire class would be kept in for an hour after school that day. When the regular school day ended, he told me that since I was absent that morning, he wouldn't punish me, so he allowed me to go home. He added that he knew that if I *had* been there I probably would have been involved in the uproar as well. He was probably right and I gave the boys a haughty smile as I left the classroom.

We had great times and a lot of fun at the various concerts put on by the Brothers. Brother Ryan was a great director and in summertime would have a huge stage built outdoors on the football field where we took part in such operettas as *The Pirates of Penzance, Capt. Van der Hamm* and others. Indoor plays in cooler weather were produced in St. Patrick's Convent auditorium and St. Mary's Hall as well as at our own school. All this, of course was before TV and full houses were the norm.

Bro. G.F. Wakeham was the author's first teacher in 1927. That was also his first year as a Christian Brother.
Holloway Studio Photo

This original Holy Cross school on Patrick Street was later torn down and replaced by a larger building, which was subsequently destroyed by fire. A much smaller Holy Cross school is now located on St. Clare Avenue.
Photo by Frank Kennedy

Staff of Holy Cross circa 1931
Photo by Frank Kennedy

Holy Cross Graduating Class 1939
Back Row: S. Stanford, C. Cahill, J. Murphy, E. Kavanagh, J. Luby.
Second Row: T. Wickham, K. Barry, K. Murphy, K. Hawko, J. Wadden, L. Madden.
Front Row: G. Baird, D. Rogers, D. Janes, G. Lannon, J. Martin, H. Martin.Unavoidably
absent: E. Finch, K. Emberly, E. Simms.
Holloway Studio Photo

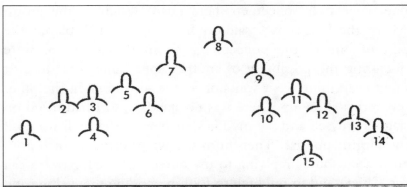

Miss Power's violin Class of 1937. Two silent bows.
Front and center, Miss Power; 1 - Jack Martin; 2 - Dick O'Brien; 3 - Fred Wadden;
4 - John Luby; 5 - Dave Rogers; 6 - Frank Burke; 7 - Charlie Noseworthy;
8 - Frank Kennedy; 9 - ?; 10 - Bill Simms; 11 - Terry Doody; 12 - Austin Ryan;
13 - Bill Luby; 14 - Pat Griffin; 15 - Len Madden.
Holloway Studio Photo

We even put on a play at the Majestic Theatre, then one of the popular movie houses. This was the story of Bernadette and the apparition of the Virgin Mary at Lourdes, France. In one scene two policemen stand guard watching the grotto where the Virgin was said to have appeared. I played the part of one of the policemen, and in the scene we were discussing the possibility of another appearance. On the first night everything went well but on the second night the other guy didn't show up. There was no stand-in, so I had to go on stage by myself and say my lines, such as, "What will we do if the Virgin appears?" Then from the wings came a voice from an unseen source replying to my question. "We'll have to call the Chief." and so on. I felt so foolish standing there alone and talking to no one. But at least there was no laughter, so we pulled it off and had a new twist to the old saying, "The show must go on." There was uproarious laughter, however, at another supposedly serious scene on the final night of the play. It had been running a week and some of the boys were becoming slightly bored. In this scene Bernadette asked the Virgin Mary to give her some sign so that the people would know she was not lying about the apparition. The Lady told Bernadette to strike the rock in front of her. The child gently struck the rock and immediately a small stream of water began flowing from a small opening. A miracle! Brother Ryan had concealed a garden hose behind the scenery and at the appropriate time, Len Madden or Gerry Reid would gradually turn on a tap to allow the gentle flow to occur. On this night the boys turned on the tap all the way and the poor child got the full force of the hose in the face. There were gales of laughter and even applause as the curtain closed on that scene. Len Madden told me recently (in 2004) that Brother Ryan never spoke to them again. Len says the boy acting as Bernadette was Mike Luby.

In 1937 Miss Teresa Power, L.T.C.L., conducted two violin classes at Holy Cross. In the junior class were twenty-two students from grades 8 and 9 and the senior class, in which I found myself, consisted of fifteen boys from grade 10. Our class seemed to make such good progress that Brother Ryan suggested it might be a good idea to have us play a number on the annual variety show. Miss Power therefore concentrated on *The Merry Widow Waltz* and we practiced that over and over. A few days before the concert, however, Miss Power realized she had a problem. Two of the boys were atrocious violin players and she knew that if she allowed them on the stage, they would ruin the show. She knew too, that to keep them off at the last minute would be very disappointing to the boys and especially to their parents who would certainly be in the audience. Very cleverly she solved the conundrum by removing the rosin from two violin bows, thus rendering them silent. The show went on with thirteen boys playing the tune and the audience thinking they were hearing fifteen. We took two curtain calls and everyone was happy.

Another very popular event was the Holy Cross Sports Day. Students competed in various games and races, for example the egg and spoon race where one holds a spoon in the mouth with a hard boiled egg on it and tries to be first to the finish line without dropping the egg; the three-legged race in which two boys run with a leg each tied together; and of course, the sack race where you stood in a large burlap bag and hopped to the finish line. We had a short game of soccer (we called it football in those days) and I was assigned goalie, being the only boy who could reach the top of the goal post. In that position I tried to emulate our local hero, Butsy Moore, who played in goal and was coach of the Holy Cross Senior soccer team. For several years they won the championship in the series, defeating such teams as the Guards, St. Pat's, St. Bon's and others. On one morning in the fall Mr. Moore and some other members of the team, accompanied by the principal, Brother Eagan, would visit the individual classrooms and display their trophy. Their visit made our day, as we knew what was about to occur. Mr. Moore would ask the principal if he thought we could have a half-holiday to celebrate the victory. Brother Eagan would then ask the classroom teacher if he could let us off for the afternoon and, of course, the answer was always affirmative, followed by a hearty round of applause.

The highlight of the sports day was the figure marching, directed by Capt. J.J. O'Grady, in which all the students marched proudly onto the field in their white shirts, gray trousers and red and yellow striped neckties, as the Mount Cashel Band played appropriate martial music. (Holy Cross colors were red and gold and later changed to green and gold). The finale of the figure marching was "The Maze", with the boys marching in single file forming a large circle on the field and gradually moving inward towards the center, then reversing direction. The result was truly a maze with each line going in opposite directions. I hated this, because being the tallest boy in the school, I had to lead the march. Most of the boys would have been proud to do this but I was very shy, very thin and over six feet tall at sixteen. Thank God I stopped growing at seventeen at 6'3. Being tall was certainly a great advantage later in life when I reached my goal of becoming a News Photographer. And thank God I got over the shyness too.

We received no sex education whatsoever in high school except one day just before graduation when Father Savin from St. Patrick's parish gave us a stern lecture on the do's and don't of sex, mostly don'ts. Our teacher had left the room before the

Highlight of the annual Sports Day was the figure marching and the "Maze".
Photo by Frank Kennedy

Holy Cross Monastery, built in 1931. Two classrooms in the basement and frightening sounds from the furnace room.
Photo by Frank Kennedy

priest began his talk, to avoid embarrassment, I'm sure. Father Savin pulled no punches and amazed us with his frankness. There were a lot of red faces in our classroom that day.

My older sister, Eileen, told me that the Presentation Sisters at St. Patrick Convent were very particular about the way their pupils dressed. She remembered one of the girls being chastised for having a dress that was too short. The nun actually pinned scribbler pages onto the hem to make the dress appear longer and cover more of her legs. She then sent the girl home to dress properly before returning to school.

After we graduated from Holy Cross, Brother Ryan continued producing much more elaborate plays in which many of the ex-pupils took part together with some very prominent actors and businessmen. A typical example was in June, 1939 when *The Mikado* was presented for a full week at the old Arena. The cast of characters boasted many well known personalities. As listed in the program, they are:

The Mikado of Japan	Mr. P.J. Dobbin
Nanki-Poo	J. F. Hennessey
Ko-Ko	G. W. Rabbitts
Pooh-Bah	R. P. Redmond
Pish-Tush	G. K. Healey
Yum Yum	Miss Julie Andrews
Pitti Sing	Mary Fennessey
Peep-Bo	Dorothy O'Keefe
Katisha	Estelle Shea

Musicals were also presented under the auspices of Holy Cross, wherein choirs of many of the city churches got together with the capable direction of Mrs. Bernard Norris and gave outstanding and well–received performances in the late 1930s and '40s. I was glad to be a member of St. Patrick's senior choir at that time and especially enjoyed the many rehearsals which turned out to be pleasant social events.

Elaborate 65-page program for *The Mikado*, performed in 1939, belonging to Mr. Len Madden, well-known retired insurance man.

chapter 6

GUNPOWDER AND OTHER AMUSEMENTS

· REACTIVATING THE SIGNAL HILL QUARRY ·

When I was ten or eleven I discovered in a cupboard in our basement a large can of gunpowder. I mentioned my find to no one in the family and since my father had an old muzzle-loader in the house, I presumed he used this powder in his earlier active years. By a happy coincidence my school buddy, Mike O'Brien, found a coil of dynamite fuse in *his* basement. His father was a professional blaster and had worked in a stone quarry at Gibbet Hill on Signal Hill. The city council used crushed stone from there for building and repairing city roads, but the quarry was now closed down. One might say we reactivated it on a smaller scale.

For many days that summer Mike and I visited the area, he with several pieces of fuse and I with a Prince Albert tobacco can filled with gunpowder. Having dug a hole about a foot deep, we then poured in some powder, put in a piece of fuse, filled in the hole with gravel and stones and lit the fuse. Then we ran a safe distance and waited. After a few seconds, much to our delight, there was an explosion with gravel and stones flying in all directions. We repeated the process until we ran out of gunpowder, after which we happily walked home. Mike lived on New Gower Street. In a few days we were back again merrily imitating Mike's father's work. Surprisingly, no one ever showed up to investigate the noise, which I suppose was not really that earth-shattering and there were no houses in the immediate area. I suppose we were lucky we had no accidents but we thought it was a lot of fun at the time.

When we had all the gunpowder used up (it must have been about ten pounds), I felt I had secretly done my family a favor, reasoning that if the house ever caught fire, and it wouldn't be the first time, then there could be a devastating explosion. The first fire occurred when my brothers, who were quite young at the time, for some unknown reason were down in the basement with a lighted candle. On the way up the stairs

The Old Quarry
Signal Hill showing the location of the quarry on the north-west side of Gibbet Hill.
Photo by Frank Kennedy

they held the candle close to some oil-skin clothes hanging on the wall beside the steps. Then they came up and went out-doors. A few minutes later the maid smelled smoke, went to the basement door, opened it and was confronted by flames. The quick-thinking young lady rushed into the kitchen grabbed a pail and filled it with water. She put another bucket under the tap and ran to the basement and began dousing the fire. After a few trips she had the fire completely extinguished. Great presence of mind. All this happened before I was born but the subject came up occasionally.

We found my father's .22 rifle and a lot of .22 shells. We had a clubroom in the basement and there was a separate door leading to the backyard. We fired one shot at a target in the basement but were alarmed at the loudness of the report and knew we couldn't do that again or my father, who was in bed upstairs, would want to know what was going on. We carefully extracted the lead bullets from the shells using a pair of pliers and dropped in one bb shot. Then with one drop of wax from a candle to keep the shot in place, we had a much less dangerous piece of ammunition. We used up the hundreds of shells in this way and had a lot of fun in the basement. The sound of the rifle shots was not too loud and our parents never knew what was going on downstairs. Much later, after we grew up, we formed the URP URP rifle club. (Unpredictable Rifle Pot-Shotters Under Rigid Policing). This was a branch of the Dominion Marksmen Association, and we had regular target shooting sessions at the Sand Pits, now the site of The Health Sciences Center. Other members included my brothers Neil and Eugene, John O'Brien, Dave Butler, Noel Vinnicombe, Nels Squires, Gene Burden and Murl Chafe. A few members, including this writer, won bronze pins for accuracy in target shooting.

Pull the Parcel

This was a frequent form of amusement in the summer months at night when the streets were fairly dark. Not practiced today with the bright street lights, we picked a dark alley just off Patrick Street where we lived. We would have a neatly wrapped parcel, usually an empty shoebox, lying on the sidewalk with a string leading in to the dark alley. When an unsuspecting passer-by reached down to pick up the package we would yank it away, usually giving that person quite a fright. One night, before we had a chance to pull the parcel, a guy kicked it and destroyed the package thus ending our fun that night. The next day we wrapped up a brick, the kind used in chimneys, and put it on the sidewalk that night. As we waited in the dark alley, two young men approached and we heard one say, "Watch this." With that he ran and made a vicious kick at the parcel. It was so hard, in fact, that the line we were holding actually broke as the brick flew through the air. As he screamed in pain we ran out of sight to the rear of a nearby house. I realized that I knew the guy. He was Mike Power, son of the well-known owner of Power's Candy Store on New Gower Street. The following day I happened to see him walk by our house and he had quite a bad limp. We stopped the game for some time after that for fear he might come looking for us.

A Ride in the Street Car

For five cents you could ride around town all afternoon in a streetcar and we sometimes did just that. For frequent travelers twelve tickets were available for 50 cents. Sometimes small children would come and ask, "Two for five, mister?" The answer was always, "OK, get aboard." The drivers, known as conductors, had a reputation of being very friendly. My

Street cars began running in St. John's in 1900, when there were no motorcars in
Newfoundland. Horse and Buggy (left) was the usual mode of transportation.
Photo courtesy City of St. John's Archives

End of the line
Water Street West near the Cross Roads was the scene of the first fatal street car accident
just two months after the inauguration of the service in 1900.
Bren Kenney Collection

brother, Neil, married the daughter of one of them, Pat Parrell. Her name was Margaret.

The streetcar tracks were laid in 1900 and there was great excitement on May 1st when Superintendent William MacKay took the first car on a run in this city of 30,000 that had no motorcars. It was a great new mode of transportation and had the horse and buggy beaten by a long shot. Public enthusiasm was somewhat diminished, however, when in less than four months, two people were killed by the trams. The first accident happened in July, on Water Street West when six-year-old Florence Baxtrom was crossing the street, became confused and stopped in the path of the car. Less than a month later, on Regatta Day, as a streetcar was going up the steep Holloway Street, the rod on top somehow became disengaged from the power line and the car ran back down out of control. The car was crowded with people going to the Regatta and 20-year-old Matthew Wadden who was standing on the back end, jumped off, was run over, and died instantly.

The route started at the Cross Roads, ran east on Water Street to Holloway Street, up Holloway then east on Duckworth to the Newfoundland Hotel, up Military Road to Rawlin's Cross and down Queen's Road to Adelaide Street and back to Water Street. Cars ran in both directions passing each other at the Railway Station and three other sidings along the route. Electric power for the system was generated at a power house constructed for that reason at Petty Harbour, which is still in operation today. The cars picked up power through pulleys on rods that were kept in contact with the wires with a spring mechanism. The voltage was 650 and the circuit was completed through the metal wheels on the tracks. There was no danger of receiving a shock if you stepped on the tracks unless you touched the overhead wire at the same time, which was essentially impossible.

I remember some years ago seeing a streetcar at the foot of Adelaide Street that would not start. There had been heavy rain and a lot of sand had washed down onto the tracks so that none of the four wheels was in actual contact with the metal. I saw the clever conductor get out and pull down the rod from the power line. Then with a poker-like tool he scraped away some sand and jammed the instrument behind one of the rear wheels thus making contact. Then he replaced the rod and got back on board. This time he was able to start the car which jumped ahead a few feet and now at least one of the wheels was actually touching the track and so the circuit was

This street car failed to make a turn near Victoria Park on Water Street on Regatta Day 1944. Another Regatta Day derailment many years earlier took the life of a passenger. Photo by Frank Kennedy

complete. He stopped, retrieved the poker and was back in business. He certainly realized that had he not removed the rod from the high voltage line, he could have been electrocuted when he rammed the poker under the wheel. He probably remembered an unfortunate conductor a few years earlier who was traveling along Queen's Road and saw a wire hanging from a pole and lying across the tracks. This man stopped the car, got out and picked up the wire, probably with the intention of coiling it up and putting it out of the way. He was killed instantly.

The first streetcars had just two seats running the full length of the car, facing each other. They seated 40 passengers. The cars were called "Double Enders", meaning they could be operated from either end without having to turn around. These cars were replaced in 1925 by more modern all-steel cars slightly larger than their predecessors. They kept running until 1948 when the last car made the final run on September 15th. By that time the streetcars had become a great inconvenience to the increasing number of motorists, since the former traveled in the center of the roadways and made a stop every few hundred yards and autos were required to stop to allow passengers to board or alight. The speed limit for the streetcars was regulated by the City Council and the maximum was 8 mph until 1937 when is was raised to 20 miles per hour. It was very exciting watching the streetcars when there was sleet on the wires. As the cars passed by there was a continuous sheet of flame trailing along as the pulley made contact with the high voltage line and there was a loud sizzling sound accompanying the fireworks.

Golden Arrow Coaches bus line replaced the streetcars and they operated from a large garage on Merrymeeting Road which is now Coleman's Supermarket. The streetcars were sold to Geoff Stirling and later advertised for sale by Doug Oliphant's Garage. The ad, which appeared in the *Daily News* on October 4th, 1948, stated that the eight cars were ideal for summer cottages, hunting shacks, or could be converted to Hot Dog stands or Taxi stands.

chapter 7

THE *VIKING* DISASTER

• MY UNCLE WAS KILLED IN THAT TRAGEDY •

I remember the day in 1931 when the sealing ship *Viking* blew up and 29 men died. One of them was my uncle, Capt. Will Kennedy, the navigator. It was Sunday March 15th and the accident happened just north of Horse Islands near the mouth of White Bay. There were several steamships at the ice-fields that year and all had kegs of gunpowder on board. It was used to blast an opening when the ships became stuck in the ice. The usual method was to attach a quart-size can of gunpowder to a pole and push it down a hole in the ice some distance in front of the ship. The explosion would loosen the ice, allowing the ship to proceed. On this trip the ship had not only gunpowder on board but dynamite as well, put aboard by a three-man U.S. movie crew from Paramount Pictures.

The previous year, American director Varick Frissell had been out there and made a movie of the seal hunt, which they called "White Thunder", a name suggested by the sound of an iceberg turning over and breaking up. However, when the film was edited, it was discovered that while there were some marvelous shots of huge icebergs, there were no pictures of one actually breaking up. Before releasing the picture, Frissell decided to go "to the ice" again with cameraman Harry Sargent and actor A.E. Penrod, and this time take along a supply of dynamite and hopefully make some icebergs turn over and break up. The actual explosion could be edited out and so it would appear the berg turned over and broke up by itself.

When the *S.S. Viking* left St. Johns on Monday, March 9 with a crew of 138 men, plus the three Americans and Frizzell's Newfoundland dog, unbeknownst to the Captain there were three teenage stowaways on board. Two were from St. John's, Edward Cronin and Michael Gardner. Most of the crew were from Brigus. The ship had been searched before leaving port and more than a dozen boys had been put ashore. But this trio was well hidden in a coal bunker and they did not show themselves until the ship was well out to sea. As the ship headed north, weather conditions deteriorated. In a couple of days some equipment had been lost overboard in the storm and on Friday, Capt. Abram Kean decided to go to Bonavista and pick up some replacements. My uncle's job then was to direct the ship in to that port. It was not unusual for a sealing ship to have two Captains on board, one in full charge and the other as navigator to plot the course. Having spent Friday night in port, they sailed early Saturday and once again headed north. That night Frissell showed the movie "White Thunder" to as many men as could be crowded into the ship's saloon and the men loved it.

By Sunday night the ship was into heavy ice just north of Horse Islands and almost jammed. Capt Kean decided to remain there, or as they say, "burn down for the night." He rang down to the engine room, "Finished with engines." That meant the engine room crew could take a long break and even take to their bunks. It was nearly nine o'clock. By morning, if the ship was really stuck, they would use some bombs. This is what they called the cans of gunpowder. Before going to bed himself, Capt. Kean instructed some of the men to get some bombs ready for the next day. Varick Frissell was horrified to see one man with a pipe in his mouth sitting on a keg of gunpowder and filling some cans. He told him to be careful or they would all be blown to hell. Many of the kegs were stored in the 'head' with the toilet and Frissell noticed some of the black powder had leaked onto the floor.

Capt. Kennedy went into the wireless room to see his friend, Clayton King. He asked if there was any news on the wire. King said no and turned off his receiver. The two then went below deck to chat with some of the men before turning in. When they entered the saloon Frissell was sitting at a table painting a sign on a piece of cardboard. King asked what he was doing. Frissell told him he was making a warning sign because the men were too careless with the gunpowder that was all over the place. Kennedy and King sat at the table and watched as he finished the sign in large letters, "NOTICE, DANGER, GUNPOWDER." Less than a minute later there was an explosion at the stern of the ship and the saloon lurched to such an extent that the men were thrown from the table and the stove overturned. Picking themselves up, the shocked men began tending the stove which was now scorching the floor

As Captain Kean rushed from his stateroom, another blast tore through the ship and Kennedy and King were blown out through a skylight. Kennedy landed on the ice with a fractured skull and King came down hard on the deck. He realized that the ship was on fire and he would have to get out of there quickly. When he attempted to stand, he was horrified to realize both his legs were broken. The fire was coming closer and he prayed, "God help me!". Using both hands he dragged himself across the deck as his clothing caught fire. While beating out the flames another explosion sent bodies flying through the air. King felt his face was very wet and reaching up his hand he discovered he was bleeding profusely from a gash in his head.

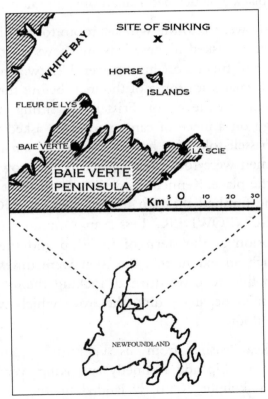

Map shows location of sinking of the *Viking*, 40 k.m. North of Baie Verte Peninsula
Map by Frank Kennedy

The fire lit up the ice around the ship and as King lay near the stern he saw a man standing out there in a pool of blood. King called out, "Who are you?" "Kennedy," was the reply, "Come out and get me." Although Kennedy was also badly injured, he was still conscious. "I can't walk." said King. "My legs are all smashed up." As he spoke there was another explosion and he lost sight of Kennedy. The wooden ship was now burning fiercely and King knew he must somehow get away. With great effort he managed to haul his body over the side and suddenly found himself in the icy water. He grabbed a piece of wood floating nearby to keep from sinking but hadn't the strength to pull himself out of the water. The American cameraman, Harry Sargent, received only minor facial injuries and was just leaving the burning ship when he heard King's cry for help. Rushing to his aid he pulled King back onto the ice.

Meanwhile on the other side of the ship, Captain Kean was taking charge of the survivors, although he was also injured when he was blown off the ship by the second explosion. The wireless room had been completely destroyed, so the best plan seemed to be to walk ashore over the ice to Horse Islands and get help. Although it was eight miles away, many of the sealers had often walked that distance hunting seals. The injured men who could not walk were carefully placed in dories that had been blown out onto the ice, and made as comfortable as possible under the circumstances. The other survivors took off for shore, pulling the dories along over the ice with them.

On Horse Islands, a small fishing village of 500 people 20 km north of the Baie Verte Peninsula, some residents were coming home from a Sunday church service when they heard a loud blast, and looking out over the ice-covered ocean they saw a ship on fire. They knew it had to be the *Viking*, as someone had recognized that ship out there just before dark. The telegraph operator there tried to contact St. John's but the office was closed until Monday, so he could not get through.

When Capt. Kean and the other men started walking to the island, they were not aware of the fate of Kennedy, King and Sargent, as they were on the ice on the seaward side of the ship. King was unconscious and when he came to, found himself on a large piece of wreckage where Sargent and Kennedy had placed him. All the other survivors were gone and King felt that the other two could easily make it to shore themselves if they wanted to, in spite of Kennedy's injuries. King couldn't remember what he said to his friend, but he remembers Kennedy saying, "Clayton, I'm not leaving you". Sargent said he was not going anywhere either.

The *Viking* sank at 2 a.m. Monday, leaving the three men in darkness as the flames were snuffed out. Sargent lit a fire with some of the wreckage and found some canned milk and other food that had been blown out from the ship's stores. By daylight many of the survivors had walked ashore and when word finally reached St. John's, three other sealing ships in the area, the *Beothic*, *Neptune* and *Eagle* were ordered to rush to the scene. The *S.S. Sagona* was in St. John's at the time and as soon as possible left port with doctors, nurses, food and medical supplies to head for Horse Islands.

The St. John's *Evening Telegram*, normally published in the afternoon, ran a special edition that Monday morning with details of the sinking, including a list of those missing. It was a sad day at our house when my father saw his brother's name on that list. Not only were they brothers, they were both Master Mariners. They had a lot in common. My father, as I mentioned earlier, was an invalid and as he lay there in bed, my mother tried to console him. "He'll turn up, Please

God," she said. He answered, "Yes, Please God he will." Then he talked about his brother. What a fine man and excellent navigator he was; how on the previous year he had gone to the ice with his friend, Clayton King, and now King was also on the missing list. There was no further news that day.

The *S.S. Sagona*, a sturdy steel ship on which my father had once been master, had reached the icefields on Tuesday, March 17 and was working her way towards Horse Islands when the lookout reported a small black object several miles to the starboard. This was 22 miles east of the scene of the disaster but the captain thought he should investigate nevertheless. He changed course and headed for the strange object. As they drew closer they saw it was a piece of wooden wreckage. With binoculars they saw a man standing on it and holding a ship's flag. It was Sargent. The wreckage had drifted more than twenty miles since the explosion and it was pure luck (or maybe prayers) that they were sighted at all. King was unconscious again with his legs badly frozen and covered with a piece of sail canvas. Kennedy was semiconscious and sitting down. He had contracted pneumonia after two nights and a day exposed to the elements. Sargent was excited with the realization of rescue close at hand and began shaking the other two to consciousness. Very soon, willing hands were helping the three men on board.

St. Patrick's Day, March 17, is historically a time of celebration in Newfoundland and when news of the rescue of the three missing men reached our house, we were all overjoyed. Our parents prayers had been answered. The *S.S. Beothic* had also picked up a dory with three missing men that same day, so it was good news all round. The *Sagona* continued on a course to Horse Islands but could get no closer than five miles before

Rescue ship *Sagona* (right) approaches piece of wreckage, all that remained after the *S.S. Viking* sank. Man holding flag is American cameraman Harry Sargent. Two other survivors are on the wreckage.
Amateur Photo

Three survivors of the *Viking* disaster are about to be picked up by the *Sagona*. At left is Capt. Will Kennedy; right, Harry Sargent; covered with piece of sail in center is Clayton King.
Amateur Photo

Rescuers from the *Sagona* pull dories filled with supplies across the ice to Horse Islands.
They brought back injured sealers.
Amateur Photo

Injured sealer from the *Viking* (in dory) is about to be taken aboard the *S.S. Sagona*.
Amateur Photo

being stuck in heavy ice. Several dories were pushed off the ship and loaded with supplies. The dedicated doctors and nurses left the ship and walked the five miles over the ice to aid the injured victims. The dories were pulled across the ice and the arrival of boatloads of food and other supplies was a welcome sight for the residents of that small village who were running short after the arrival of 118 unexpected visitors.

The next day 103 survivors walked to the *Sagona*, taking the injured men in the dories back to the ship. The steamer remained in the area for a few days searching for bodies before heading back to St. John's. Unfortunately, Kennedy's condition worsened in spite of the intensive care given him by Dr. Patterson, Nurse Berrigan and the other medical personnel on board. He passed away just as the *Sagona* was about to enter the Narrows on the early morning of March 24.

One of the young stowaways was also killed in the explosion. He was Edward Cronin and was a first cousin of the renowned writer and historian, Dr. Paul O'Neill, who incidentally is a first cousin of this writer. The bodies of director Frissell and actor Penrod were never recovered and the Newfoundland dog, Cabot, met the same fate as his master. Back in St. John's, Clayton King had his two legs amputated, and was the first Newfoundlander to drive a motorized wheelchair. He became a successful dry goods store owner. Harry Sargent went back to New York virtually empty handed, his equipment and film having gone down with the ship. The title for the film, "White Thunder" not now being appropriate, was changed to "The Viking" and was released under that name. It didn't do well at the box office, however. It seems that as far back as the early '30s, even before the Animal Rights people became involved, the Americans did not take kindly to swarms of Newfoundlanders out on the ice floes killing these lovely furry creatures. Nevertheless, more than seventy years later the picture has now become a classic, being the first feature film made in what is now Canada and also the first American sound production shot at a foreign location. Thanks to the efforts of Dr. O'Neill and other members of the Historic Sites Association, the film is now available on VCR cassette.

The actual cause of the disaster was never determined, presumably because any witnesses had been killed in the initial explosion.

chapter 8

A FUNNY THING HAPPENED

The Kittens

When my sister, Eileen, was a young girl and I was an even younger boy, she allowed our cat, Sal, to sleep with her in her bedroom on the second floor of our home. We didn't know that the cat was about to have kittens. Our mother knew, of course, but we were never told the facts of life and would never know about impending births until after the fact. One dark night the entire household was awakened by the cries from Eileen, "Mom! Mom! Come in and turn on the light!" My mother responded, "What's wrong Eileen?" "Sal is in my bed with a lot of mice," she cried urgently. "Don't worry about it, honey, that's all right. Go back to sleep," said mother.

"Are you sure everything is all right?" insisted Eileen. "I'd like you to come and turn on the light so I can see for myself." Mom replied, "Yes, everything is alright. Now go to sleep. That's the good girl. Goodnight honey." "Goodnight Mom." Most of us went back to sleep.

Next morning our mother went into Eileen's room and was surprised to see only Eileen and the cat in the bed. "What happened to the 'mice'?" Mom asked. Eileen's reply. "I threw them out the window." Sure enough when I went down and opened the back door, there were these four or five little kitty corpses strewn about the back steps. Eileen didn't let the cat sleep with her after that.

The Chicken Legs

Many years ago my older brother, Neil, was manager of MacDonalds' Fruit Store on Long's Hill. One day a regular customer came in and went to the frozen food section and picked up a package of chicken legs. She showed them to my brother and asked, "Are these hind legs?" My brother, thinking it was just a joke went along with it and answered, "Oh yes ma'am, these are hind legs." The lady said, "I'll take them." She paid the price and without cracking a smile left the store. Neil was dumbfounded and often wondered what she thought of him when she realized what a faux pas she had made. He didn't find out though, as she never came back to the store again. Maybe she was used to buying frozen rabbits.

Beware of the Dog

When I was a teenager we had a rat Terrier named Mac who loved riding around in my brother Eugene's car. Eugene could go to a movie and leave the dog in the car. No problem. Mac could curl up asleep in the back seat for hours. One evening when Eugene came out of a movie the front door of the car was ajar. But the dog was still in there. Someone must have attempted to get into the car during the show and was scared off by the barking. When the car was due for a lube job, Eugene brought it down to Terra Nova Motors. They were located at the rear of Hotel Newfoundland, the present site of the Aliant building. My brother forgot about the dog in the back seat, brought the keys in and was told to come back in the afternoon. When he walked back around four o'clock he was a little surprised to notice the car was parked in exactly the same spot where he'd left it. When he went to the service department he was told they couldn't do the car as that damn dog would not let anybody near it. The service manager had given the keys to a mechanic and told him to bring in the car. After a few minutes the mechanic returned and said he couldn't get the car started. The service manager haughtily remarked, "Ah boy, these English Cars are a bit tricky (it was a Morris) give me the keys. I'll bring her in." In a few minutes he was back and not too happy. "You nuisance," he said, "I can see why you couldn't get that damn car started." Eugene was told to come back the next day *without* the dog.

Mac turned out to be a good burglar alarm, as my brother Jack found out much to his chagrin. One night Jack was out at a house party that lasted until 2 a.m.. Our good mother didn't want any of us staying out past midnight and told us so in no uncertain terms on the few occasions we did that. When Jack arrived home after two in the morning, he had no key and decided to sneak in through a basement window. After successfully pushing his way in as quietly as possible, he was walking towards the basement stairs in the dark when he slammed his head into a radiator pipe. The sickening thud woke the dog and the dog woke everyone in the house with his excited barking. We heard my brother say, "It's only me, Mac, be quiet!" But the damage was done. Not only did Jack have a nasty bruise on his forehead but he got a stern lecture from mother as well.

Our milkman often had problems with the dog. My mother would leave an empty milk bottle inside the unlocked back door and when the milkman reached for it, Mac rushed towards him, growling and barking. It seemed the dog didn't appreciate anyone taking something out of his house even if he did leave something better in its place. It got so bad that finally my mother would put the empty bottle outside the door. I remember sometimes in winter the milk would freeze and push up a cone of hardened cream two inches high with the bottle cap on top.

Our one-eyed terrier, Mac, and friend. No need for a compass.
Photo by Frank Kennedy

Wetting a Line

My aunt Maude MacPherson had no children but would often take us trouting. She was an expert angler and liked fishing in Second Pond and Fourth Pond in the Goulds. When my much older brother, Eugene, bought the car I mentioned earlier, he would take us farther afield up the Southern Shore and the Salmonier Line. We usually went trouting every Saturday in the summer and stopped on our way along at the Infirmary, or "Poor House," as it was then called, for a can of worms for ten cents. When we entered the building we would have to see a Mr. Walsh. One day we told him we wanted two cans. "What?" he cried, "Two cans?!" With that he collapsed to the floor in a dead faint. It gave us quite a start but as a nurse rushed to his aid, another resident told us consolingly, "He's not used to being asked for two cans." Then he got us our bait and my brother Neil and I were hustled out of the building as Mr. Walsh was being revived.

One day we were driving along the Salmonier Line looking for a likely spot when we saw a nice large pond by the side of the road. We decided to give it a try. When we started getting our gear ready we noticed just up the road an elderly man in a garden mowing hay. We walked up to him and asked if there were any trout in this pond. He answered, "No, no trout there. A guy caught them all yesterday." We thanked him and said we would try anyway. We were excited at what he'd told us. From our experience, if someone caught a lot of trout one day, the next day there would be lots of trout back in the same spot. However after three hours wandering around the pond we finally conceded the old guy was probably right. We didn't even get a bite.

On another occasion an acquaintance of ours who lived around the bay told us there was a nice big pond behind his house where there were lots of trout and we should come over some time if we liked trouting. On Regatta Day that year we drove around to his house and he was delighted to see us. Sure enough there was this nice large pond a few hundred feet back from his house. He told us he had just come back from the pond and had caught eight trout. He told us to be careful not to walk on his trouting pole which he had left on the shore with the bobber out in the water. He said he leaves the baited hook out in the pond all the time. This was very encouraging news for us. Eight trout! We enthusiastically

'Bait Depot'. The old three story infirmary, commonly known as "The Poor House," was located on Sudbury Street. This was where we bought our worms for trouting. In 1965 the building was torn down after all the residents were moved to the new Hoyles Home on Portugal Cove Road.
Photo by Frank Kennedy

Ed Bruce pedals by Windsor Lake in 1939.
Photo by Frank Kennedy

baited out hooks and cast out, and out, and out. We were there all afternoon and didn't even get a rise when finally our friend came back to check his line. Nothing there either. We mentioned the eight trout he had told us about and asked him if he had caught them that morning. "Oh no," he replied, " I caught eight trout so far this summer."

Our dog Mac loved going with us any time we went trouting and would often jump in for a swim. What we really liked about having him with us was that no matter how far we wandered from the road, when we decided we had had enough, all we had to say was, "OK Mac. Let's go home." He would take off at once and lead us back to the car, stopping every hundred feet or so for us to catch up. No need for a compass with him around. When he was three years old he was hit by a car near our home and had to have an eye removed by Dr. Furneaux, the well-known veterinarian. Mac lived twelve happy years after that until the 24th of May one year, which was usually our first day fishing. After running around gleefully all that day he suffered a fatal heart attack. The vet told us that during the previous year, he had aged several dog-years and the exertion was too great for his little ticker. We were sorry to lose our pet of so many years but it was some consolation to know that he died doing what he liked best, going trouting.

Mr. Fitzgibbon

I remember Mr. Fitzgibbon as a fine neighbor in the 1930s and '40s. He was elected City Councilor in 1949 and served for eleven years. Another councilor, I'll call him George, was a member of an organization that at that time was reputed to be very anti-Catholic. Certainly George openly expressed his dislike for anyone or anything connected to that denomination. At one council meeting George announced that the following week he would be bringing up a certain bill for consideration of the members. Fitzgibbon was very much against this proposal and when the meeting ended he engaged in a heated argument with George, trying to dissuade him from bringing in the bill. George told Joe he might just as well save his breath as no matter what happened he was going to bring in the bill anyway. Finally, in desperation, Fitzgibbon threatened, "If you bring in that bill I will have Archbishop Roache go in and bless Windsor Lake and you will be drinking holy water for the rest of your life!" The bill was never introduced.

chapter 9

THE RIOT
OF 1932

• PRIME MINISTER SQUIRES
BARELY ESCAPED WITH HIS LIFE •

I remember the riot on April 5, 1932, when Liberal Prime Minister Sir Richard Squires was almost killed as thousands of people swarmed Colonial Building. Civil unrest was rampant and on that very day the War Veterans formed a large troop of Special Police to patrol the city and restore peace. I remember seeing them walking the streets in pairs wearing big black armbands with the initials "SP" for "Special Police". We called them "Squires' Protectors".

Squires was voted in as Prime Minister in 1929 in spite of the fact that during an earlier stint as PM in 1923 he had been considered by many to be a crook. That year the Auditor General reported $100,000 missing from the Liquor Control Department. An independent financial expert, Thomas Walker, was brought over from England to investigate and found that indeed, at least $20,000 of government money went to Squires illegally. He also noted, among other irregularities, a transfer of $43,000 to the personal bank account of Squires from the

Bell Island Mining Company. No charges were ever laid.

Newfoundland voters have a short memory. Or at least they did in 1929, for that year Squires was voted in once more and it seems he was soon at it again. This time, according to his Finance Minister Peter Cashin, he was siphoning money from the War Veterans Pension Fund and using it to pay off government expenses, and taking $5,000 a year for what he termed legal fees. One of Squires' cronies, Dr. Alex Campbell, was being paid a salary as Minister of a department that didn't even exist, a Department of Immigration. That man was also accused of failing to file income tax returns.

The financial devastation of the Stock Market crash of 1929 in New York had filtered down to Newfoundland, and the government was in desperate straits. The colony was deeply in dept and could raise no more loans. Squires even tried to sell Labrador for one hundred and ten million dollars but there were no takers. The Great Depression had raised its ugly head and unemployment and poverty were widespread. Cashin resigned as Finance Minister, condemning Squires for his skullduggery. When Squires announced spending cuts for public services, teachers' wages and war veteran's widows' allowances, that was the last straw! Something would have to be done to get rid of this man. A public rally was called for Monday, April 4 at the Majestic Theatre to decide how to handle the matter. Among the reporters covering that rally was the editor of the weekly newspaper *The Watchdog*, owned by Squires. At one point this man asked permission of the chairman, Eric Bowring, to say a few words. Getting the nod, he began to defend the Prime Minister. The crowd would have none of that. Amidst booing and heckling two burly men punched him and threw him out of the building. His name was Joey Smallwood. As the meeting progressed, four men were elected as a delegation to go to the House of Assembly next day and demand an investigation into the charges of corruption against Squires and his government.

Everyone knew there would be trouble at the Colonial Building the next day and my brothers and I were not allowed to go over there. We were young children and our parents feared for our safety. In fact one ten-year-old boy was treated for injuries suffered during the ensuing riot. The city merchants declared a holiday for April 5 so that the employees could join the big procession which formed up at the Majestic Theater, near the foot of Theatre Hill (now Queen's Road). In the early afternoon the parade moved off, led by the Guards' Band and members of the Great War Veterans Association. In charge were Messrs. H.A. Winter and W.E. Godfrey. Winter had admonished the marchers to "keep it peaceful". By the time the parade reached Rawlin's Cross it had grown to over three thousand people – men, women and children – and at the Colonial Building another seven thousand greeted them. Thirty policemen stood at the steps guarding the premises with 'billy-knockers' in hand. Four Constabulary mounted policemen opened a path through the crowd to let the delegation get to the building. The band played a martial air as the four men passed through the entrance. The door was closed behind them. The House of Assembly was in session and the Prime Minister questioned the legality of a delegation interrupting the proceedings. There was a half-hour delay as Squires sought legal advice.

Outside, the huge crowd grew restless. The band played *The Ode to Newfoundland* and that had a calming effect, but not for long. Some impatient people began shouting. The mounted police, fearing there would be trouble, rode their horses to the foot of the steps. There they were attacked by the mob. Constable Jim Lake was hit with a stone and fell unconscious to the ground and ended up in hospital. Another man was dragged from his horse and sustained serious head injuries from which he never fully recovered. He spent the rest of his life as a patient in the Waterford Hospital. Word came that the delegation was about to exit the building so the crowd quieted down to hear the news. There was almost complete silence as the massive door opened. As the four men came out the door was slammed and bolted. The announcement was made that they had failed. That did it. All hell broke loose. The mass of humanity surged towards the building and up the steps. The thirty policemen with their batons were overwhelmed and an attempt was made to break open the front door.

Civil unrest was rampant in St. John's in 1932. On April 5, thousands of angry citizens swarmed the Colonial Building during a session of the legislature and Prime Minister Sir Richard Squires barely escaped with his life.
A 2-160 Courtesy of "The Rooms" Provincial Archives Division

Inside the legislative chamber, when the commotion was heard, the house quickly adjourned. Squires moved into the protection of the adjoining office of the Speaker of the House with his wife, Lady Squires, who was an elected member, and some other MHAs. Also there was Joey Smallwood who had been covering the house session for *The Watchdog*. They barred the door. Very soon rocks came crashing through the windows and the Prime Minister and the others had difficulty avoiding the flying glass. They realized to their dismay that the building was under siege. All the windows were smashed and the picket fence adjoining Bannerman Park on the western side was knocked down and pickets torn off and used as weapons against the police. In an effort to quell the riot the Guards' Band struck up a martial tune and announced they were going back to the Majestic. Few people heard them and as they marched out of the grounds very few followed them. The mob was out for blood. Having failed in their attempt to break open the front door they attacked the door on the western side and succeeded in forcing it open. Once inside, the hoodlums wrecked everything in sight, pulled out office furniture and files and set them on fire on the grounds. The legislative librarian, a Miss Morris, had an apartment on that floor and her upright piano was dragged out into Bannerman Park. There, someone played a few tunes before smashing it to pieces and throwing it into the fire. Police finally forced the rioters out of the building and caught a boy stealing the ceremonial mace, while another boy made off with the Speaker's sword. The crowd were out of the building, but they were not going anywhere. They knew Squires was still inside and were determined to get him. The MHAs left the building unhindered but fourteen people were taken to O'Mara's drug store just up the road, to be treated for cuts and bruises.

As darkness began to close in there came a knock on the door of the speaker's office. It was Edward Emerson, one of the members of the opposition. "Are you in there, Sir Richard?" he asked. No answer. Again he asked, "Are you in there, Sir Richard? We have come to escort you out." A female voice answered, "We are not coming out." "My God!" said Emerson, "Are you in there too, Lady Squires? You had better come out right away. They are trying to set the building on fire." That was true. Two attempts were made but were unsuccessful. The door opened and Lady Squires was escorted out and disappeared unnoticed through the crowd.

Squires always wore glasses and usually a hat but now he removed the glasses and pulled someone's cap down over his forehead and managed to sneak out unrecognized through the side door to a waiting car. The car moved slowly through the crowd, then across Military Road and had just entered Colonial Street when someone shouted, "There he is! There's Squires in that car!" A human stampede took place and the car was quickly surrounded and stopped. From a nearby doorway came a shout, "Come in here, Sir Richard." It was the home of a Mrs. Connolly. Some historians claim it was No. 60, others say No.66. As Squires left the car, more shouting was heard. "Get him!" "Drown the bastard!" "Down to the harbour with him!" With the help of a half dozen self-appointed bodyguards Squires got into the house. By a stroke of luck, two clergymen, Rev. W.E. Godfrey and Father Joseph Pippy were right there and stood in the doorway blocking access. After a slight delay they were roughly pushed aside and several men burst into the house. In the meantime Squires had gone out the back door, over a fence and in through a house on Bannerman Street and made a safe getaway.

The mob, realizing their plan had been thwarted, sought vengeance. Hundreds went to the West end liquor store, broke in and passed out bottles of liquor, bucket brigade style, until the shelves were empty. Another segment went to the East end store where they had difficulty breaking down the door. The problem was solved when someone produced an axe, chopped down a telephone pole and used it as a battering ram. This store was also cleaned out. On the way along several Chinese establishments had windows broken.

As mentioned earlier, the Great War Veterans Association immediately formed an *ad hoc* troop of special police and with the help of the local force, order was soon restored. Squires went into hiding for some time, but soon an election was called and he brazenly ran again and was soundly defeated by Fred Alderdice's Progressive Conservative. Party. The final count was P.C.s. 34, Liberals 2. Squires never ran again and dropped out of public life and retired to his home at 44 Rennies' Mill Road, where he passed away in 1940 at the age of sixty.

chapter 10

DUFFY'S GROCERY

· WATER, FIRE, AND BANANA BUGS ·

I spent a lot of time during my childhood at Duffy's Grocery. In fact, I was run over by their horse-drawn delivery wagon when I was eight years old. The store was located on the corner of Patrick and Pleasant Streets just opposite our home. I recall the vacant lot and the start of construction of the two-story building. The second floor was to be the living quarters for the Duffy family. I remember when the workmen left the site at lunch time, my little friends and I would go into the partly finished building and play Cowboys and Indians. There were no stairs leading to the second floor, only a ladder and we enjoyed climbing up and down that ladder. The construction men often chased us away and warned us not to come back. No doubt they were afraid we would get hurt. One day when they arrived back I was on the second floor and got my foot caught between two pieces of lumber and couldn't escape. I still remember the man saying, "Now I got you!" I was so frightened, I peed in my pants. I thought he was going to kill me. Much to my relief he just moved the lumber so that I could get free, and told me to "Git!". I lost no time running home.

When the building was finished, the next door neighbor informed Mr. Duffy that whereas the wall adjoining his property was exactly on the boundary line, the eave encroached upon his property and would have to be removed. Legally, of course, he was right, but what a wonderful neighbor! Mr. Duffy forthwith had the eave removed and several years later, because of rainwater running down inside the clapboards, a lot of rot ensued and the complete wall had to be replaced.

On another corner of our street stood the home of Mr. Arthur Johnson, the well-known insurance man and his two young sons, Evan and Paul. Evan grew up to be a noted musician and Paul became not only the president of Johnson Insurance Inc., but founder of the philanthropic Johnson Family Foundation, which has done so much outstanding work for the community over the years. Mrs. Johnson's father, Capt. Jolliffe, a retired Master Mariner, also resided there. Running the full length of the house was a large deck and often Capt. Jolliffe walked back and forth for exercise. My father would tell us "The captain is walking the bridge again to-day."

When Andrew Duffy opened his family grocery store, his first customer was my older brother, Neil, who was waiting on the doorstep that morning at eight o'clock and brought a half pound of Tip Top soda biscuits. When we grew up, Neil always referred to me as 'my kid brother' although I was nearly a foot taller than him. Of course, I referred to Neil as 'my big brother.' Duffy's made deliveries with the help of a horse-drawn four-wheel wagon with a seat for the driver, Ern Gollop, a kind and gentle person. Mr. Gollop often let me ride with him on his rounds. Scattered throughout the city were large horse

Andrew Duffy's Grocery (right) after a snowstorm in 1939. At left is the home where renowned businessman Paul Johnson spent his childhood.
Photo by Frank Kennedy

The Duffy building in 2004, now a furniture store. Still no eave.
Photo by Frank Kennedy

troughs and it was interesting seeing the horse quicken his pace when he spied one of these. There was one at the junction of Hamilton and New Gower Streets, another on Duckworth Street at the foot of Bates' Hill, one on Cavendish Square near the Newfoundland Hotel, and one at the top of Prescott Street near Rawlin's Cross. This was the last one to be removed from the city streets and is now in Bowring Park. Dogs were catered to as well with these drinking fountains. Underneath the large trough were three miniature troughs close to the ground so that passing dogs could refresh themselves. All were connected to the city water system and had fresh running water.

One nice sunny day at Duffy's, Mr. Gollop had the wagon loaded with boxes of groceries to be brought to a coastal boat at the dry dock premises. There were so many large wooden cases that he had to take out the seat to make room for the cargo. I asked him if I could come along and he told me there was no seat, but if I wanted to sit on top of the boxes, then it was okay. Of course I gladly climbed aboard. Mr. Gollop told me to be careful as there was nothing to hold on to. We went down Patrick Street and down Power Street with no problem. At the foot of Power Street, however, he made a sharp right turn and I fell off the wagon and onto the front wheel. This carried me to the ground and passed over my stomach as I lay face up on the pavement. Before I could get up, the rear wheel rolled onto my stomach and I heard Mr. Gollop shout "Whoa! Whoa!" The horse did stop but the rear wheel was on my stomach, pinning me to the ground. Mr. Gollop jumped off the wagon, ran around to the rear wheel and attempted to lift it from me. He couldn't do it so he yelled, "Gid-e-up! Gid-e-up!" The wagon moved ahead and he picked me up. The street had been freshly tarred and my white shirt and gray short pants were a mess. I don't remember what Mr. Gollop said then but I took off and ran home. When I got there I was feeling sore and sick, so I went straight to my bedroom, took off my dirty clothes and lay down on the bed. After a short while I was horrified to hear Mr. Gollop's voice from the open front door calling out, "Mrs. Kennedy, Mrs. Kennedy, did Frank come home?" My mother said she thought she heard me come in and wondered why he seemed so concerned. When he told her what had happened they both came rushing up to see me. I was afraid I would be scolded for ruining my clothes. Instead, of course, my mother was very sympathetic and both she and Mr. Gollop were thankful I was not badly hurt. Had the wheels passed over my chest, almost certainly some of the little ribs would have been broken by the heavily loaded wagon.

I did get a severe scolding some weeks later, though, thanks to another visitor. I had found an old tobacco pipe my father had rejected and I secretly filled it with some of his Prince Albert tobacco. I took it down to my friend Mike O'Brien and we went behind his aunt's house on Pleasant Street and lit up. We passed the pipe back and forth excitedly for a while, enjoying the blue cloud we were creating on that calm day. After some time it wasn't much fun anymore. In fact, I began to feel sick. Suddenly we heard a window opening and Mike's aunt put her head out and shouted, "Frank Kennedy, I'll tell your mother on you!" With that we stopped our activity and went home. There, my mother looked at me and said I didn't look well and wanted to know if I was all right. I told her I was feeling sick, and then sat down on a couch in the kitchen. She sat with me and put her arm around me to comfort me. Just then the back door opened and Mike's aunt appeared and announced, "I just saw Frank and Mike O'Brien smoking a pipe down behind my house." As I stood up, my mother said, "No wonder you're sick," and gave me a slap on the behind as I left the room.

Since there were several hundred horses trotting around the city daily, including many from nearby settlements, the city hired professional pooper-scoopers. These men patrolled the streets with their wide brooms and shovels and two-wheel containers shaped like an upright barrel. The streets were kept reasonably clean but in our area they were not paved and on dry windy summer days, there was a problem with dust. Mr. Duffy diminished this problem somewhat by sending me out on the sidewalk with his garden hose attached to a tap on the outside of the store. I really enjoyed spraying the streets in all four directions, as far as I could reach. When I had finished and everything was soaking wet I was supposed to coil up the hose and put it away. However, one day as I was happily spraying, a fire truck roared past me down Patrick Street with siren screaming. Looking down the street I saw a cloud of black smoke coming up behind Wesley Church. I thought our school, Holy Cross, was on fire and I dropped the hose and ran. As I passed the church, I saw, with a dab of disappointment, it was not our school after all, but the fire seemed to be in the western end of Water Street. Indeed it was, for Marshall's Garage and Showroom was going up in flames. Before I reached the foot of Patrick Street I heard a loud explosion and after arriving at the scene there were several other blasts as gas tanks of cars inside the building blew up and wreckage flew through the air. It was the first 'big fire' I'd seen. Little did I realize that later on in life I would spend over forty years with the media covering fires and other news events. It was two hours before this conflagration was brought under control and I strolled back to Duffy's store. Mr. Duffy was not happy to see me. He didn't mind my going to the fire, but leaving the hose on the sidewalk was something else. While I was gone, a wholesaler delivered a barrel of beef and rolled it over the hose, smashing the nozzle. I stayed away for a few days after that.

The city council members were not oblivious to the dust problem and had a large truck which we called "The Sprinkler", which sprayed water on the dry streets. It resembled a large oil truck with two special spouts on the rear that sprayed water the full width of the street. The machine usually moved along slowly and we often ran behind it and into the spray. It was very refreshing on a hot summer day. The big excitement was when the truck was being refilled at a city fire hydrant. There was one right in front of our house and we really enjoyed sitting on our front steps and watching the action. The driver hooked up a big hose and turned on the hydrant. The highlight came when the tank was full. There was no gauge and the water gushed up in the form of a big geyser from the top of the truck, sometimes soaking the operator as he strove to shut off the water.

Back at Duffy's, as the years passed, Mr. Gollop retired, the horse died and Mr. Duffy bought a car, a coupe with a rumble seat. He had that seat removed and a long wooden box built in so that the car now looked like a small pickup truck. A fine young man, Jack Fagan, was hired as the driver to deliver groceries. Also working in the store were two ladies, Ina Ebsary and Mary Breen. Mary was the sister of the well known CBC producer, Derm Breen, now deceased. When these ladies were not busy serving customers or filling grocery orders, they filled and weighed one- and two-pound brown paper bags with such staples as green peas, white beans, split peas and rolled oats, which came in bulk form. The bags were tied with twine and placed in bins, thus saving time for future orders. Mrs. Duffy (Jennie), a very likeable lady, also worked in the store occasionally when she wasn't busy raising her lovely daughter, Joan. Mr. Duffy was a fine gentleman and a hard worker. One day he caught me rooting around the straw in a crate of bananas, presumably attempting to steal one. He warned me that such activity could be very dangerous as sometimes there were banana bugs in the straw and their bite was fatal.

I was a teenager by now and although still attending school, I sometimes worked part-time especially in summer, helping with the deliveries. Jack Fagan and I really hit it off and he made me feel important by telling me to watch out for emergencies and always be ready to pull on the hand brake. It seemed as if I was the co-pilot. In the 1930s, cars didn't have four wheel hydraulic brakes, just two wheel mechanical brakes. This meant a lot of pressure had to be applied to the foot brake in order to stop a car in a hurry, Hence the hand brake was called "the emergency brake," and would lock up the rear wheels. One day we were driving along Water Street West when a young boy darted out of Victoria Park and straight across the street directly into our path. Jack swerved the car and I pulled hard on the hand brake and we screeched to a stop just inches from that lucky little boy. Jack said "Good work, Frank!"

In the 1930s the city dump was located where Cornwall Crescent sits today and that was just outside the city limits. There was very little actual garbage dumped there. What rests underneath the houses on that street are thousands of tons of ashes from the hundreds of coal stoves, fireplaces, furnaces and so-called hall stoves throughout the city. Practically all kitchen waste was burned in the kitchen stove. In fact the man who collected the refuse daily was called 'the ash man'. One day when Jack and I were at the dump depositing some waste material, we noticed a cloud of smoke in the East end of the city. Deciding to investigate, we drove back and found the chapel in Belvedere cemetery on fire. I remember seeing the firemen pouring water on the wooden tower as it burned fiercely and started collapsing. The firemen dropped their hoses and ran for their lives as the steeple came crashing to the ground in a heap of burning wreckage. No one was injured but the pressure of water in the hoses caused them to wriggle out of control and many of the bystanders had an unwelcome drenching. The lovely building was burned to the ground and never replaced. And speaking of fires, in the 1930s there were more than a hundred fire alarm boxes on telephone poles throughout the city. All had numbers. At the central fire station there was a large fire-bell mounted on a tower and when an alarm came in the number of the box was sounded manually on this bell, which could be heard all over town. For example, if the box was No. 312, the bell would sound – ring, ring, ring, pause, ring, pause, ring, ring. The city telephone directories listed the locations of the alarm boxes with their numbers and anyone could find the location of a fire by checking the directory, as I often did. The number was actually sounded three times. An "All Out" signal was also given by a series of two strikes of the bell. There was no box number 222. This system was a carryover from the days when only a skeleton crew was on duty at the station and if an alarm came in, the off-duty men would know where to report. That same bell, which weighs more than a ton, is now in place atop the new fire station at the corner of Harvey Road and Parade Street. I remember walking along Duckworth Street one day when a car burst into flames. There happened to be an alarm box right at hand, just outside the old city hall, so of course, I sent in an alarm, which was responded to very quickly.

Jack Fagan taught me how to drive although we didn't own a car. On Saturday nights when it was dark, we had to make a delivery to Mason's store near Mundy Pond, among other places, and Jack would allow me to drive although I was only sixteen. The following year my brother Eugene bought a car; although he couldn't drive, he thought that if I got my license then I could teach him. And that is exactly what happened. Jack Fagan took me over to Fort Townsend for the test. It was not very difficult in the '30s to get your driver's license in St. John's. There was no written test and no oral test, all you had to do was drive around town for ten minutes with a policeman in the front seat with you. Some of these guys would ask you as you passed the Basilica "What time is it?" If you looked up at the clock in the tower you would fail the test for taking your eyes off the road. The only other tricky part was Longs' Hill. Halfway up you had to stop the car and take off again without letting it slip back. There were no automatic transmissions then, so if you let the car run back or stalled the engine, you failed the test and were told to practice for another week. I passed the test on the first try and both Eugene and myself were very grateful to Jack for his help. He was really a swell guy! Of course I took my time teaching Eugene, who owned a convenience store on Water Street, and while he was working I had the car. I dragged it out as long as I could but finally had to admit he was now a fully qualified driver and ready for the test. Needless to say he passed with no problem. Nevertheless, he still let me use the car while he was working. It was about this time that I took a full time job as customs clerk with Clancy & Company and that ended many happy years of part-time work at A.V. Duffy's grocery. Before leaving there, one Saturday night Mr. Duffy gave me $1.50 and on the following Monday I went to Tooton's, the Kodak store and bought my first camera, a Baby Brownie, for $1.20, no tax. This was a far cry from the twenty thousand dollar movie camera that would be assigned exclusively to me thirty years later at the CBC.

chapter 11

AUNT MARY MALONE

· SURVIVOR OF THE "ROARING TWENTIES" IN CHICAGO ·

My aunt Mary and her husband Maurice lived ten years in the crime-ridden city of Chicago in the United States and after many hold-ups, robberies, break-ins and a shooting, they gave it up and moved back to Newfoundland. I'm glad they did, for I spent some of the happiest days of my childhood on their farm 'in the country' on Oxen Pond Road.

Aunt Mary told me a lot about life in Chicago in the 1920s. Robberies and murder were commonplace and it seemed there were crooks with guns everywhere. Uncle Maurice ran a small A & P supermarket with my aunt as cashier. One New Year's eve three gunmen entered the store and ordered: "Everyone into the back room!" Looking at my aunt he commanded her: "You stay here!" Poking his revolver into her side he told her to open the cash register. She obeyed and he told her to sit on a nearby orange crate. As the crook emptied the drawer, one of the others noticed the gold

Mary (Kennedy) Malone

watch chain hanging from my uncle's vest pocket and demanded to see the watch. As he removed it from his pocket he said, "You don't want this old watch. I've had it since I was a boy." The robber looked at it and replied, "I guess you're right, it's no good to me. It's too old". and handed it back. Two years later this very watch probably saved his life. The trio took the money and several cartons of cigarettes and made a clean getaway. A few days later, however, they were caught red-handed at another holdup and were arrested. It turned out that their ring-leader was a former manager of another A & P supermarket.

One night when the store was closed, a lone robber broke in and was helping himself when he was spotted by a policeman outside. As this lawman stepped through the doorway, the crook drew a gun and pointed it at him but the policeman was quicker and shot him dead on the spot. Another night as aunt Mary stood with the cash drawer open, she looked up to see a man pointing a gun at her. He told her to step aside. She did so and he laid the gun on the counter and started scooping up the cash with both hands. My aunt reached for the gun but he grabbed her hand and said' "Don't do that, lady!" She drew back. When he had taken every cent from the till, she suggested, "You might at least leave us some change." He paused, looked at her and put back $2.84 in coins. The last straw came one night when a black man entered and fired point blank at Mr. Malone and he fell to the floor. The would-be robber must have scared himself, for he turned and ran away without taking any loot. As it happened, Uncle Maurice was only slightly bruised. The bullet hit his gold pocket watch and bounced off, almost certainly saving his life.

That was it for the Malones. They packed up and headed back to their quiet, comfortable, beautiful, safe home on 12 acres of land on Oxen Pond Road, just outside St. John's at that time. For a few summers my two first cousins, John Kennedy, Bren Malone and myself spent a week of our holidays there, not to mention numerous happy day visits. Bren's brother, Bill, was the father of the renowned comedian, Greg Malone. Although they had none themselves, they certainly loved children, especially aunt Mary who spent hours amusing us and taking us on walks and picnics. The Leary's river ran through their property and they built a swimming pool there and we really enjoyed that on many a warm summer day. One day we three boys came across a large bird on the property. It seemed unable to fly so we went back and told uncle Maurice about it. He came and picked it up and put it into a carton. The bird was about the size of a hen and he drove out to the old Memorial College on Parade Street in his Ford sedan with wire spoke wheels. We tagged along in the back seat. At the college we were told it was an Eastern Bittern, not a common sight in Newfoundland. They usually frequent marshes, are fairly well camouflaged and if danger threatens they will often stay still, apparently hoping they will not be noticed. This is why uncle Maurice was able to pick it up. We were told that if we brought it back to the farm and released it, it would probably fly away. That is exactly what happened. Back home when we opened the carton the bird jumped out, made a few steps and took off and flew slowly away towards Oxen Pond as we waved goodbye.

The Malones had a beautiful flower garden in front of their home and in the middle, a big patch of gooseberries. And I mean BIG. Aunt Mary asked us to help pick some gooseberries and gave each of us a bowl. We were on one side of the bush and she was on the other side and we couldn't even see her. She promised there would be a prize for the boy who filled his bowl first, and told us to keep whistling as we picked. If anyone stopped whistling, she would say, "Someone's not whistling." It was only after our bowls were full that it occurred to me the reason my aunt wanted us to keep whistling – you can't eat berries if you are whistling. Anyway, the race was declared a three-way tie and each of us received a prize, a nice dish of gooseberries and cream. One night one of our little friends

'Keep whistling'. Aunt Mary Malone in the gooseberry bush with her nephew, this writer, as a teenager.

from up the road was playing with us in the house and by ten o'clock aunt Mary suggested it was time for him to go home. He left but was back in a few minutes saying he was afraid to go home in the dark. There were no street lights, of course, as this was outside the city at that time. Aunt Mary said "Don't worry, I'll come with you." Then she went into the kitchen, picked up a large carving knife, waved it in the air and said "Let's go." They went. Ten minutes later she was back smiling. It was not really pitch dark, she said as there was a full moon. They met only one man and he crossed to the other side of the street when he saw them coming.

That year, on our last night on the farm, Aunt Mary thought it would be a nice idea to have a big bonfire. We spent all day gathering old wood, blasty boughs and other trash and when it was dark, aunt Mary set fire to the big pile. It was a great bonfire and on that calm night the flames went twenty feet into the sky. A lot of neighbors came and enjoyed the spectacle and some of aunt Mary's friends, the Cofields, who lived nearly a mile away on Freshwater Road, saw the glow and thought the house was on fire and came rushing to the scene. There were no telephones, of course, to call and inquire as to what was going on. They were happy to see what was actually happening and they stayed and enjoyed the sight. It wasn't until the fire died down that we could get close enough to roast marshmallows and a good time was had by all.

Much later, in the '50s, St. John's extended the city limits and appropriated nearly all the land, leaving just a small lot where the house stood. That house still stands today and is now No. 46 Oxen Pond Road, and lies on the corner of the newly created Hatcher Street, which runs through the exact location of Malone's big barn where we often played 'Hide and Seek' in the hayloft. A four-lane highway runs through the property parallel to Leary's river, Prince Phillip Drive, and that road completely wiped out the section of Oxen Pond Road leading up to Nagle's Hill.

Aunt Mary and Uncle Maurice moved away once again; this time to Toronto. They never returned.

chapter 12

AROUND
THE
TOWN

Mass Panic at St. Patrick's Church

St. Patrick's Church was always filled to capacity on Good Friday afternoon, with hundreds standing at the rear of the building. On one such day, which I well remember, panic broke out when someone idly removed the valve from a radiator near the back doors and a huge cloud of steam filled the air. People thought it was smoke and someone yelled "Fire!" The rush for the exits was instantaneous. There was panic in the aisles. A friend of mine, Frank Burke, lived directly opposite the church on Patrick Street and was just leaving his house when he witnessed the incredible sight of dozens of people jumping out the windows. This was before the stained glass windows were installed and ordinary windows which opened outwards were in place. People jumped out and ran away.

Back inside, I, a teenager, was literally frightened to death. I didn't know what to do and to make matters worse, I was up in the choir gallery with only one way out down a winding staircase, so I just stood there in the pew, in shock I suppose, until the priest, Father Kitchen (later Monsignor) realizing what had happened, rushed up into the pulpit and uncharacteristically shouted repeatedly that there was no fire, only steam from a radiator. This calmed us down somewhat and the rush for the doors soon abated. There were no serious injuries and the service continued with the church only half full. That was a Good Friday service that was remembered by many parishioners.

During the ten years I attended high school at Holy Cross, there were four Masses celebrated at St. Patrick's church every Sunday morning. The 9:30 a.m. Mass was the children's mass and one side of the church was filled with girls from nearby Presentation school, while on the other side sat the boys of Holy Cross. In every tenth pew on our side sat a Christian Brother keeping an eye on the boys and the same with the Presentation Sisters on the left. After Mass we had to go back to school for an hour of religious instruction. At that time, Catholics wishing to receive Holy Communion were required to fast from midnight the previous night. When we got back in school after Mass, the Brothers allowed those boys who had received Communion to leave at once and go home to breakfast. Some of the boys who didn't mind fasting, would 'go to Communion' just to avoid the one-hour instruction.

Bowring Park

My good friend Jack Browne and I often walked to Bowring Park from our homes on Patrick Street, across the trestle and in the railway track. It was only two miles, but if you had five cents you could board a bus at the Railway station, on a load-and-go basis, and ride to the park entrance. For a few years a steam coach, similar to a streetcar but twice as long and powered by an enclosed steam engine, made trips every summer day. This luxury ten–minute ride cost ten cents. I still remember the shrill sound of the whistle as the coach approached the Waterford Bridge Crossing. One summer a locomotive pulled a regular passenger car to the park and ran all the way back to town in reverse. The fee was also a dime per person for a one way trip. It was the shortest train in the history of the Newfoundland Railway. On very busy weekends, taxicabs also made the run from the railway station, sometimes crowding seven or eight kids into a car for the five cent fare. Some private citizens even got into the act and spent an afternoon doing the same as the taxis.

'Five-cent bus ride'. In summertime this bus carried passengers from the railway station to Bowring Park. For us the fare was five cents; for adults, a dime.

This steam coach traveled from the Railway Station in St. John's to Bowring Park in the 1930s. Fare was ten cents. Coaches were not cost effective as they needed 3 persons to operate them: an Engineer (driver), a fireman and a conductor.
Photo courtesy Railway Museum

At the park the train stopped at a small station. Sometimes we put a one-cent coin on the railway track and when that eighty-ton locomotive rolled over it, the copper coin was flattened to a very thin disk. We didn't do that very often because it ruined the commercial value of the coin. For one cent you could buy a jaw-breaker or two banner caramels or as many as eight 'common candies'. Jaw-breakers were individually-wrapped chocolate covered toffee, one and a half inches square. Banner caramels were unwrapped toffee cubes, also chocolate covered, and 'common candies' were small hard candies of various sizes, shapes and colors composed mainly of sugar. A one-cent coin was slightly larger than a quarter, exactly one-inch in diameter. They were never referred to as 'pennies.' A penny was two cents and that coin was larger than the present-day two-dollar coin.

Once inside the park, the big attraction for us was the boat pool, now referred to as the duck pond. There were three wooden rowboats under the supervision of a park guide. He allowed a certain number of children on board. The boats were nearly always overcrowded but no serious accidents ever occurred and anyway, the water was only two feet deep. With ten or twelve kids on board, the guide would select two of the bigger boys to do the rowing, one oar each. This was a very much sought-after position in the boat with the question "Can I row the boat, mister?" being asked repeatedly. I was often selected, being a bit tall for my age, and that was a great thrill. There were often dozens of children waiting on the small wharf for their ride around the pool and after about twenty minutes, the guard called a boat back. There being three boats, there was a quick turnover of passengers. Of course these little excursions were free.

There was a large swimming pool built right on the Waterford River and that was very popular on warm summer days. Being on a river, the water was continually being changed but unfortunately, housing developments further up the river caused pollution in the water and the pool had to be closed and drained. A new modern concrete pool was built on the north-western end of the park and is still in use today. Miles of trails and footpaths meandered through the park, into woods, through lovely displays of flowers and on the banks of two beautiful rivers. I remember how much we enjoyed wandering through the tall stately maple and birch trees on the banks of South Brook.

The original fifty-acre park was donated to the city of St. John's in 1914 by Sir Edgar Bowring and was officially opened by the king's uncle, His Royal Highness Prince Arthur, on July 14 of that year.

Flooded. The old swimming pool in Bowring Park in flood after a heavy rainstorm.
Photo by Frank Kennedy

Newfoundland's First Traffic Light

The first traffic light in Newfoundland was installed at Rawlin's Cross in St. John's and went into operation on May 13,1936. I was attending school that year and kept a diary. In it I note that on May 17, I walked the mile and a half from our house just to see this new marvel. Big deal. The light was operated manually by a policeman in a tiny booth on one corner of the street. There were only two lights facing each way, red and green, no amber, and were mounted on a single wooden post in the center of the intersection with the words, "KEEP LEFT" clearly visible. In 2004 there were more than sixty intersections in the city controlled by automatic traffic lights.

When the first motorcar was brought into Newfoundland by Robert Reid in 1903, St. John's residents had already been riding around town for two years in streetcars. This new car was no 'tin lizzy' either, but an expensive Rolls Royce from England. For the next century, tens of thousands of cars, busses and trucks were imported into the colony. It was rumored in the late 1930s that the American car maker, Henry Ford, offered to build a paved road across the island if he could bring in his cars duty free. The offer is said to have been turned down by the Commission Government on the basis that we already had a railroad from St. John's to Port aux Basques, and were badly in need of the revenue generated by the importation of autos. Thirty years later, that road was completed at a cost to the Federal and Provincial governments of $250, 000 000. They promised to "Finish the drive by sixty-five" and did just that, albeit some sections were poorly constructed and quickly deteriorated. The highway was officially opened on July 12, 1966, by Prime Minister Lester Pearson at the halfway point just west of Gander.

The section of the TCH leading out of the city is Kenmount Road and I remember when we were young lads, that dusty road was so narrow that cars slowed down to pass each other. We often rented bicycles from Pike's Cycle Shop on Springdale Street for ten cents an hour and pedaled in that road and out Topsail Road, back to town.

Newfoundland, being a British Colony, maintained the "Drive Left" rule of the road for several decades until the late '40s when the Newfoundland Light and Power Company announced the pending closure of the streetcar service. This public transportation service would be replaced by busses and the only busses available in North America were built for "Drive Right" conditions. That being so, the rule was changed

Newfoundland's first traffic light went into operation on May 13, 1936 at Rawlin's Cross in St. John's. It was operated manually by a police officer in the tiny booth at right in photo. No amber light.
Photo courtesy City Hall, City of St. John's

First two motorcars to arrive in Newfoundland were these Rolls Royce models owned by Robert Reid, Jr. and his brother Harry. This was in 1903, and by that time St. John's citizens had already been riding around in street cars for two years.
Photo courtesy CBC Archives

on Jan 2, 1947. Fears were expressed that the changeover could result in head-on collisions but only one was reported in the city, with no serious injuries. The transition took place in midwinter, so traffic was not heavy and the drivers adapted to the change with little difficulty. But not the horses. There were hundreds of horse drawn carts and wagons in the city and the animals had been so accustomed to keeping to the left, that a lot of near-misses resulted. The *Evening Telegram* reported the changeover in the issue of Jan. 2, 1947, as follows:

> *"After twelve hours of driving to the left, at noon today, St. John's could be said to have taken to the new driving rule of the road, which was issued in at the stroke of midnight, like the royal swans took to the boat pool in Bowring Park last summer.*
>
> *To prevent traffic snarls at Rawlin's Cross, one of the heaviest congested areas in the city, several policemen were doing duty in case their services were required.*
>
> *On the whole, motorcars and trucks were going slower than usual early this morning, but as the day wore on, the novelty wore off, engines were fed more gas and the tempo of driving was quickening.*
>
> *One of the underlying reasons for the change in the driving rule was the expected merger of the city bus and street car transportation system, which will be succeeded by electricity driven trolley busses. It is desirable for passengers to disembark from a bus directly on the sidewalk instead of in the path of traffic, and the only trolley busses obtainable are those from the States and Canada where drive right is the law."*

Of course the trolley busses were never brought in. They would not be very practicable in St. John's, their use being limited to the streets where the wires were strung.

I remember when I was very young, there were no cars on the city streets in winter. With the first heavy fall of snow, that was it. No more driving. The horses took over. There were no snowplows, but the streetcars kept running thanks to the "sweeper". This was a special rail car with two immense circular brooms, angled to throw the snow to one side of the street. It carried no passengers and cleared the tracks so that the streetcars could continue operating. There were many delays in the service, especially on Water Street, when horses and sleds traveling on the tracks had difficulty getting out of the way, due to the pileup of snow on each side.

After World War I, a huge 30-ton British war tank was shipped to St. John's and for years was parked in front of the Court House on Water Street. In the early '20s it was driven around the main streets in winter to flatten the snow and make traveling easier for horse and pedestrian traffic. Most of the horses had small sleigh bells attached to their harness and the tinkle, tinkle, was a very pleasant sound as they passed by on a nice winter day.

The fire department transferred their hoses, ladders and other fire fighting equipment to sleighs in winter and several horses stood by in a stable-like enclosure at the rear of the fire hall. At the sound of an alarm, these animals were trained to trot out and stand under the shafts and harness of a sleigh. In less than a minute the rig was lowered, the two part collar was snapped in place by a fireman and they were off to answer the call. In summer, we enjoyed watching the ladder truck responding to fires. This was a very long vehicle almost fifty feet in length. We called it "the six-wheeler" and it required two drivers. The rear wheels were steered by a man sitting on top of the stack of ladders. When rounding a corner, he turned the rear wheels in the opposite direction so they would not

Water Street, looking west from Prescott Street in 1938. Very little traffic.
Photo by Frank Kennedy

The old six wheeler, looking down the ladder. Note no windshield. Not built for speed.
Photo by Frank Kennedy

run in over the sidewalk. The six-foot steering column passed vertically down through the ladders and had to be taken out before any of the ladders could be removed from the truck. There was no windshield on the machine but being so cumbersome, it was not really intended for any great speed. The rear wheels were solid rubber and that must have made the ride uncomfortable for that man up there hanging on to nothing but a large steering wheel, as the contraption rattled along the unpaved streets. No power steering either. In rainy weather, well, let's not think about that.

Many motorists stored their cars in garages during the winter and usually had them jacked up slightly so that the tires were off the floor. It was believed that the weight of a car resting on the tires all winter could cause the rubber to deteriorate to such an extent blowouts might occur the following summer. Our good neighbor, Mr. Graham Day, the well-known radio repair expert, stored his convertible in Mr. Duffy's garage, just across the street from our back door. The garage was never locked and we often played there pretending we were driving the car. It was a lot of fun and we were amazed at how easy it was to turn the front wheels while making appropriate engine noises with our mouths. We longed for the time when we could sit behind the wheel of a car and actually drive it. It was much later that we discovered the wheels were not touching the floor.

In the early '30s snow plows appeared, enabling cars to operate all winter long with the help of skid chains. Snow tires were not generally available for cars. Eaton's Winter Catalogue listed "Road Gripper Chains" @ $3.25 per pair and extra heavy "Trojan Chains" @ $5.65 a pair. Sometimes a link broke in the short section running over the thread and the bar, as it was called, would strike the fender with every revolution of the wheel, producing a clank, clank sound. As the winter wore on and the skid chains wore out, this annoying noise became more prevalent and certainly clashed with the pleasant tinkle of the sleigh bells. I once picked up a skid chain near our house and was delighted to receive a fifty cent reward from the owner who had advertised the loss in *The Daily News*.

TROJAN CHAINS
$5.65 Pair

Ad in Eaton's 1937 Catalogue
Trojan Chains $5.65 Pair

A traffic holdup occurred in our area on a regular basis when herds of cattle were driven through the streets. About once a month, fifty or sixty cows trotted up Patrick Street and up Pleasant Street on their way to Lester's field. They arrived by train and were being driven by cowboys walking along with big sticks, but no horses. Cars were forced to stop, of course, to let the animals pass by. From our front steps we enjoyed watching the action. Sometimes a cow would wander onto the sidewalk, but was quickly prodded back to the street by an alert handler. After some grazing at the field, the animals were "processed" and sold to the various city butchers.

chapter 13

MY FATHER, CAPT. NICHOLAS KENNEDY IV

Yes, the fourth. His father, grandfather and great grandfather were all ship's captains and all named Nicholas! It would not be too farfetched to say the sea was in the Kennedy blood. My father's brother was also a Captain, William Kennedy of the *S. S. Viking*, and his two uncles, John and Terrance, were Master Mariners. By an odd twist of fate, my father's grandfather was born at sea, and if that had not happened, my father would never have been born. Nor would I. Here's what happened. The original Nicholas Kennedy was born in Ireland in 1782 and was married about 1806 to Grace Young, an Irish lass twenty years of age. The Kennedys made their living from the fishery, but for several years that industry had been declining. Consequently, Nicholas and his brother decided to take their families and migrate to the United States, where the cod fishery was thriving. Many fishermen went along with them. They set out in their two sailing vessels in February 1807. The voyage would take several weeks and half way across the Atlantic, Grace gave birth to a son. The weather was bad and the seas

Capt. Nicholas Kennedy
Holloway Studio Photo

stormy and in consideration of the health of the new baby and his mother, it was thought wise to put in to the nearest port, which was in Newfoundland. Nick's brother sailed on towards Massachusetts, but when he and his family landed at Crocker's Cove, near Carbonear, the fishery was so good that they stayed. Baby Nick grew up, met and married Julia Kennedy (no relation) and their son was my father's father. If the baby had not been born at sea, he would never have met and married Julia, but would almost surely have grown up in the United States and probably married there.

Creeping Paralysis

I mentioned earlier that my father developed what in the 1920s was called 'Creeping Paralysis'. Today it would probably be known as Multiple Sclerosis. My earliest recollection is seeing him at home pushing a kitchen chair ahead of him and using it as a walker. I would have been about five years old and although he lived sixteen more years, I can never remember seeing him walk unassisted.

The first sign of the disease came when he began staggering slightly while walking. Some friends understandably accused him of being intoxicated. He had always used a walking cane for style and found that two walking sticks helped him maintain his equilibrium for a while, but after a few weeks he had to resign his position as ships' Captain. He sought help from many physicians and traveled to New York and was examined by specialists but they told him nothing could be done to stop the progress of the disease. Being a religious man he even made a pilgrimage to the shrine of St. Anne in Quebec where many cures had been reported, but to no avail. He was totally resigned to his fate and returned home. In a few weeks his legs became completely useless and he was unable to stand up and was thus confined to a chair or bed. For a while his arms were not affected and he could feed himself and pass the time reading, etc., but gradually the insidious illness took over and finally he could not move his hands at all. That disease was well named! Thankfully and surprisingly to us, his mind was never affected, nor the five senses, especially the sense of touch. I remember sometimes on a summer day as he lay there in bed he would ask for someone to come and drive that "damn fly" away. The insect was walking on his hand and the tickling sensation was driving him crazy, but he could not move a finger.

My mother read newspapers to him every day. He liked to keep up with current events and if we forgot to turn on the radio for the Gerald S. Doyle news bulletin every night, he was not happy. He could still read, of course, but he couldn't hold the paper. Every spring during the sealing season there was a special Sealing News broadcast at 10 p.m. reporting the number of seals taken by the various ships and the location of the steamers. I remember one night when the latitude and longitude of one of the ships was given, my father laughed. I asked "What's so funny, Pop?", which is what we all called him. "Well," he replied, "If that's the location of that ship, she's up in the woods." He certainly was a very qualified Master Mariner. He was also a very patient man. Not once in all these years did he complain. At no time did he fall into the "Why me, Lord?" mode.

During my childhood he told me many stories, as did my mother, and I think it would not be inappropriate for me to relate some here, as they were an integral part of my growing up in St. John's.

Stranded on Labrador

In late autumn of 1895, Nick Kennedy (my father), at the age of eighteen, with his parents and the rest of the family, were marooned on the coast of Labrador with the distinct possibility of starving to death as the harbours began freezing over. At that time it was customary for hundreds of Newfoundlanders to take their families "down on the Labrador" every year for the summer fishery. They sailed in their own schooners with enough provisions to last the entire season. They lived in big houses built decades earlier for that purpose. The Kennedys also had a bunkhouse for the regular fishermen that accompanied them, and a barn for the cow, other livestock and hens they always brought along. As the men caught and salted the codfish, the women spread and dried it in the sun.

In early May that year three Kennedy brothers, Nick, (my grandfather), Terence and John, all ship captains, took their families, including twenty-eight children, and sailed from Crocker's Cove, Carbonear, in their three schooners. Also on board were maids to help with the housekeeping and cooking, as well as several regular fishermen who were paid no wages but would share in the proceeds of the total catch when it was sold in the fall. They were called sharemen. Capt. Nick knew from previous experience that cod were in abundance off Labrador and had made arrangements with a friend, Capt. Dan Pumphrey, to pick up his family and the sharemen in September on his way home. Pumphrey would be fishing farther north and Capt. Nick figured that by not having to bring back the entire family and the other fishermen, there would be room on his schooner for a few more thousand pounds of fish. He would send the fully loaded ship back with the first mate in charge and wait for Pumphrey to pick them up. He would also take home some of Pumphrey's catch. Back in Harbour Grace the earlier arrivals got a better price for their product.

Summers in Labrador were traditionally sunny and warm and 1895 was no different in Sloop Cove just north of Hamilton Inlet where they lived. The fishery was carried out from trap skiffs and dories, brought to the fishing grounds on the decks of the schooners. Young Nick, a budding captain himself, helped his father with the navigating during the five hundred mile voyage from home. He and two other brothers, Peter and Lar, who were teenagers, helped with the fishing. While the men and women worked hard, Nick's four daughters and the two younger sons enjoyed themselves playing games, beachcombing, trouting, jigging cod and picking berries with their nineteen first cousins. They found swimming in the ocean very invigorating and were delighted the water was so warm. They had no fear of being bothered by strangers. This isolated community had no other inhabitants.

Five-year-old Mary had her own special "boat" and played in it for hours every day near the water's edge. It was actually her mother's wooden washtub and Mary loved it. They found a cave in the nearby hills and often had boil-ups there, sometimes cooking vegetables they stole from uncle Terence's garden. Life was good in Sloop Cove that year. There were fresh eggs every day from the flock of hens they'd brought along and fresh milk from contented goats and the cow. In late summer, there were plenty of jams from the blueberries, bakeapples and other wild berries the children had picked, and a good supply of potatoes, carrots, turnips and cabbage, thanks to having planted these vegetables early in May after they had set their traps. Everyone was happy, especially the children who were enjoying an extended summer vacation.

By mid-September, as the days grew shorter and the nights grew colder, it was time for the Kennedys to pack up and go home. The first ship to set sail was Capt. Nick's. It was now fully loaded with a bumper cargo of dried salt fish. Pumphrey had been sending down skiff loads of fish during the summer and this was packed on board as it arrived. Most of the family's clothing and bedding was put aboard to save time when Pumphrey arrived in a few days. As planned, the first mate, a competent sailor, took the ship back home leaving one trap skiff which the Kennedy family would need to board Pumphrey's ship. The voyage home usually took two weeks. Days later when brothers John and Terence were about to weigh anchor, they tried to persuade Nick to come along with them. They hated the idea of leaving the family isolated. Nick was adamant. Pumphrey had promised to pick them up and that was that and they knew the ship was farther north anyway. He didn't want Pumphrey coming in and finding them all gone. Two regular fishermen remained behind, but the others took advantage of the offer of an earlier ride home.

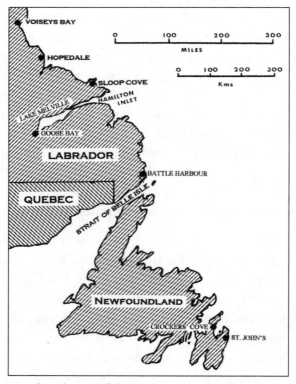

Map shows location of Sloop Cove in Labrador, where the Kennedy's were marooned in 1895, 500 miles north of their home in Crocker's Cove.
Map by Frank Kennedy

Although thirteen people stood on the shore and watched and waved as the two ships sailed away, there was a feeling of loneliness and uncertainty in the minds of some of the adults. Maybe thirteen was an unlucky number.

The Kennedys had fifty pounds of salt fish, one hundred pounds of flour and other small grocery items on hand and that should provide plenty of food for three days waiting for Pumphrey. On the day of the expected arrival, Mrs. Kennedy sat looking out over the ocean as seagulls flew lazily overhead and gentle waves washed the shoreline. The weather was cool but she was comfortable in her home-knitted woolen sweater. To her great delight she saw a sail on the horizon. It was Dan Pumphrey's ship and it was sailing down the coast about six miles offshore. She waited anxiously for the vessel to turn to starboard and head in to the cove and was puzzled when this did not happen. As the schooner moved farther away she ran to find her husband and tell him the bad news. Nick told her she must be mistaken. She couldn't have seen a ship passing down the coast, as Dan's was the only one up there and he would be coming in to pick them up. Margaret Kennedy was frantic and was absolutely certain she had seen a ship. Nick could see no ship but just to be sure, he climbed to the top of a nearby hill and was amazed to see a sail just before it disappeared in the distance. He was flabbergasted. How could Pumphrey be going home without them? But he obviously was doing that and in another week or two the cove would be frozen over, making rescue impossible. It would take Pumphrey's ship at least two weeks to get home and find out the terrible mistake he'd made, and by that time it would be too late to return. Marconi hadn't been around yet, so there was no possibility of wireless radio contact.

Nick and his wife discussed the grim situation. They had very little food left, considering thirteen mouths to feed. They had shotguns for hunting small game, but not much ammunition. All their heavy clothing and most of their bedding had already been sent home. Even now for the past two days, it was so cold outside the children had to play indoors. They had been abandoned for some incredible reason and now faced starvation or freezing to death in the wilderness unless they moved. But where could they go? Nick knew of four or five native families living twelve miles away at Emily Harbour and decided they should try and reach them. However, to walk there through the barrens and brush in the cold, late September weather would be impossible. There was not even a trail or path and the children had only light summer clothing. Their only hope was the trap skiff, which fortunately had been left behind. There was no time to waste. It could snow any day now this far north, so the next day they put their remaining provisions aboard the boat and had the smaller children lie on the bottom where they covered them with the remaining bedding. Shortly after dawn they began rowing south, the three men and the older boys taking turns with the oars. There being very little space left on board the skiff, Mrs. Kennedy put her pots and pans into her washtub and had it towed behind. They would be making no great speed, so there was no problem there. The problem was with young Mary. She wanted to get in "her" boat herself and be towed behind. Never mind the pots and pans! Many years later she told me she still remembered going into a tantrum about that. Her father ordered her to "Shut up and lie down!" in the boat. She was my aunt Mary featured in Chapter 11. Before leaving the cove they left a note in a conspicuous location in the house, noting where they had gone in the unlikely chance someone should come looking for them. The skiff was heavily loaded and they

Fishermen in Crocker's Cove prepare fishing nets for the annual Labrador summer fishery (circa 1912). Third man from left: James Butts; fourth: George McCarthy; Eighth: Jack Clark
Photo courtesy Provincial Archives of Newfoundland and Labrador

Julia (Kennedy) Malone with husband Tom. At the age of seventeen she was almost forced to marry an Inuit hunter when her family was marooned in Labrador in 1901.
Photo by Frank Kennedy

made slow progress in the chill north wind. Fortunately the sea was calm and they managed to reach Emily Harbour before darkness set in.

The native people were surprised to see a skiff with a few adults coming ashore, and were amazed when several children popped up from the bottom of the boat. Luckily everyone spoke English to some extent and the visitors received a warm welcome. The Kennedys found there were four homes, each with one family. One of the families moved in with the other three and gave their house to the new arrivals. It was not much more than a shack with a roof of sods and a large open fireplace, but at least it was warm even if there were no beds. The natives were glad to receive some of the flour and salt fish and shared their own food with the visitors. Nick and Margaret prayed for a rescue, but as the days dragged on, there were occasional snow flurries and the harbour froze over so it seemed they might have to spend the winter in Emily Harbour. On fine days Nick and the two sharemen went hunting with the natives, but game was scarce and usually they brought back only enough rabbits and birds to make soup. The families intermingled, helping each other with house work and cooking, etc., but one day unexpectedly, the chief hunter (we'll call him Joe) announced he wanted to marry Julia, Nick's seventeen-year-old daughter. This presented a big problem. She knew if she turned him down outright this humiliation could be disastrous, especially now that all their provisions were used up and this man was supplying most of their food. She shyly told him how honored she was that he held her in such high regard but as she was only a young girl, he would have to talk to her father. And talk to her father he did, and Capt. Nick realized as well that here was a delicate problem. Talking as if father to son, Nick told the suitor that it was customary in their society for young ladies to be fully grown and fully developed and to carry on a longer courtship before being married. Maybe he could wait a while. The young hunter gave Julia beautiful furs in the expectation of winning her over. After three weeks the situation became very tense. Joe became irritable and could not understand why Julia did not want to marry him. After all, he was now supplying most of the food for her entire family. He was a good provider and a good man. Julia was afraid she might have to marry him regardless, for her families' sake.

In the meantime, fifteen days after passing Sloop Cove, Dan Pumphrey's ship sailed into Harbour Grace, a few miles from Crocker's Cove. This is where the cargo of fish would be sold. The Bishop of Harbour Grace, His Excellency, Ronald McDonald, was on hand at the wharf to meet the Kennedy family and welcome them back home. He was astounded to find they were not on board. Equally surprised was Dan Pumphrey when he heard the family was not home already. He was emphatic about the fact he thought Nick and the family were coming home with the brothers and claimed this was a monumental misunderstanding. The incensed bishop immediately contacted Newfoundland Prime Minister Sir Robert Bond demanding a steamer be sent to rescue the castaways. It so happened that Captain P. Delaney of the sealing steamer, *Grand Lake*, who was a good friend of Skipper Nick, heard of their plight and offered to go to Labrador and bring them back. The *Grand Lake* was capable of breaking through thick ice and Delaney was familiar with the area, having fished there earlier himself.

In three days the *S.S. Grand Lake* was butting its way in to Sloop Cove. Two men went ashore and found the note, and the ship headed south. In Emily Harbour Nick Kennedy spotted smoke on the horizon. Were their prayers being answered? They were.

Very soon the steamer was grinding its way through the ice floes and closing in on land. When Kennedy recognized his old friend on the bridge he was so excited he actually waded out into the icy water up to his waist to greet him. Mrs. Kennedy cried tears of joy and the children literally went mad, jumping and screaming at the thought of their rescue. As they were leaving, young Julia thanked the native chief for all he'd done for them and with tears in her eyes told him that perhaps someday she might return. But they both knew in their hearts that this would never happen. Joe was not a happy man. He told her "You can have everything I own if you will stay and marry me." Julia declined a final time.

When the *Grand Lake* arrived back in Harbour Grace, once again Bishop McDonald was there along with hundreds of others to welcome the Kennedys. This time they were not disappointed. Some government members were not happy, though. They wanted an inquiry held. After all, that steamer had been taken out of service for over a week and the rescue operation was quite costly. Capt. Pumphrey was summoned to court in Harbour Grace and found guilty of abandonment of thirteen souls on the coast of Labrador. He pleaded a misunderstanding. Capt. Nick believed him but the judge found him guilty of criminal carelessness and gave him a heavy fine and a severe reprimand.

Capt. Nick never took his family to Labrador again. Two years later they moved to St. John's. Julia later married Thomas Malone, a grocer, and they are the grandparents of the renowned comic actors Greg and Benny Malone. Julia's younger sister Mary married Maurice, the brother of Thomas and, as mentioned above, some of her interesting life's story have been told else where in this book.

Favourite Sailing Vessel Destroyed by Fire

During his sea-going career, my father commanded at least four sailing vessels and eight steamships, including the *Terra Nova*, *Prospero* and *Sagona*. His favorite sailing ship was the *Ich Dien* and when she was destroyed by fire, he was quite upset, especially since he had paid a watchman to look after the ship in his absence. The watchman shirked his duty, resulting in her complete destruction. In the early 1900s, Crosbie and Company had a large fleet of sailing ships. In his book, *Newfoundland Ships and Men*, Andrew Horwood states "There was no doubt when the *Ich Dien* came to Crosbie's she was the queen of the ships. Captain Nicholas Kennedy was appointed to command her..." And command her he did, making several trips to South America with cargoes of salt fish in drums and bringing back shiploads of rum and molasses. In the fall of 1908 the ship was chartered to Baird Gordon & Co. to take another load of fish to Brazil. The ship was tied up at Baird's premises, just down from the present site of the Court House, when the Baird premises caught fire. A crew had not yet been hired for this trip and my father had paid a watchman to look after the vessel while he was at home but that man was nowhere to be seen when the fire broke out. My uncle, Capt. William Kennedy, happened to be on board his ship nearby and realizing the danger, boarded the *Ich Dien* and untied her, thus allowing the ship to drift away from the wharf. But it was too late, the ship had already caught fire and after dropping anchor in the stream, Kennedy managed to jump into a small rowboat which, fortunately, had been tied to the railing. In his book, Horwood continues "The blaze that enveloped the *Ich Dien* was more spectacular than was the fire at Baird's premises. There were no firemen to turn water on the barquentine. When the sails and yard arms ignited, the vessel in her dying moments was something to remember." My father could never locate that watchman again. Probably a good thing for both of them. After the fire he was put in command of *The Jean*, another fine ship, on which he would take his wife on their honeymoon voyage to South America.

Love at First Sight

My father met my mother through a good friend of his, James O'Neill, father of the renowned historian and author, Dr. Paul O'Neill. Both men were living in St. John's at the time and Mr. O'Neill invited my father to come and spend his summer vacation with him at their parents home in Bay de Verde. It was there that James introduced his sister, 27-year-old Nellie, to my father. It was love at first sight and they were married in the autumn of 1908; James was best man. Nellie was the only daughter of well-known merchant John O'Neill, Esq. The wedding in that small town was really a three-day celebration, not unusual in those days, and was reported in the *St. John's Free Press*. Oddly enough, the quaint account details the presents given by the groom to his bride and the bridesmaids.

WEDDING BELLS

KENNEDY – O'NEILL

Bay de Verde was in fete on Wednesday, the 2nd instant, in honor of the wedding of Miss Nellie O'Neill, only daughter of John O'Neill, Esq., the respected merchant of this town, and Capt. N.J. Kennedy of St. John's, one of our most successful master mariners. Guns were fired and flags floated gaily in the breeze. Strings of bunting stretched over the houses at different vantage points, and Old Sol shed his genial rays as if to cast a ray of happiness over the happy couple. The ceremony was performed at the Church of the Assumption by Rev. Fr. Donnelly, in the presence of a very large number of people. The bride looked charming in a dress of white silk, with veil and a wreath of orange blossoms, and entered the church leaning on the arm of her father. She was attended by Misses Maud O'Neill and Charlotte Moore, and little Miss Mary O'Neill as flower girl. The groom was supported by Messrs. J. O'Neill and T. Kennedy. Dr. McDonald presided at the organ and played The Wedding March. *After the ceremony, the bride and groom, accompanied by a very large number of guests, proceeded to the residence of John O'Neill, Esq., where an enjoyable night was spent. Rev. Father Donnelly, in a felicitous speech, paid high tribute to the bride, who is one of the most popular young ladies in musical and social circles. The Rev.gentleman also spoke in kind terms of the groom, who, although young in years, had, by energy, attained a prominent position. Graceful speeches were also given by Messrs. D. O'Neill, Jas O'Neill and T. Kennedy. The groom replied in suitable and happy terms. The groom's present to the bride was a splendid gold bracelet, and to the bridesmaids, gold lockets with long gold chains attached. The bride and groom drove to Old Perlican Thursday morning and spent their honeymoon there, returning here Friday evening. A grand ball was held in St. Joseph's Hall on Thursday night in honor of the event, and on Friday night a reception was held at Mr. O'Neill's residence, at which nearly one hundred guests took part. Dancing, singing and music were enjoyed until 4 a.m. The happy couple left by Saturday's* "Ethie" *en route for St. John's. The* S.S. Ethie *was decorated with bunting, and McCarthy's Hotel at Carbonear, and other residences were also covered with flags. The presents to the bride were numerous and costly, testifying to the esteem in which she is held by her many friends, who unite in wishing Mr. and Mrs. Kennedy every happiness in their future life.*

Bay de Verde, Sept. 7, 1908

A few days after the wedding in 1908, Capt. and Mrs. Kennedy posed at Vey's Studio in St. John's.
Vey's Studio Photo

As stated above, the official honeymoon was just one night plus two days, but the real honeymoon began a little later after they reached St. John's a two month cruise to Brazil on a sailing vessel with the groom as Captain and his bride the only woman on board. My mother often spoke of that wonderful voyage. She remembered sitting on deck, arm in arm with her new husband, the ship gently sailing across the equator on a beautiful moonlit night. The romantic strumming of a guitar, played by a member of the crew at the bow of the ship, and the pleasant rustle of sails in the soft tropical breeze provided a musical backdrop. An occasional flop-flop announced the arrival of another flying fish as it hit a sail and fell to the deck, thus providing a tasty entrée for next morning's breakfast. These fish have a greatly enlarged pectoral fin enabling them to emerge rapidly from the water and sail through the air at a great speed for up to 200 yards.

My mother remembered how every day around noon, my father and the first mate got together to calculate the ship's exact position, the mate with a chronometer and my father with a sextant, an optical instrument for determining latitude. With my father looking at the sun through the sextant and the mate concentrating on the time-keeping instrument, there was complete silence for a minute or two until suddenly the mate shouted, "Now!" My father wrote something down in a notebook, according to my mother, and then went to his cabin with the mate and herself trailing along. On a large chart, he marked the distance the ship had traveled in the last twenty-four hours. Sometimes the distance was a half inch and if there had been a strong northerly breeze, it might be a full inch. On some days they hardly moved at all. After some weeks of this procedure, one day my father, having marked the chart, announced "Tomorrow we'll see land." Next day my mother was glad to hear a crew member shout from a masthead "Land Ho! Land Ho on the starboard bow!" It was Pernambuco.

The distance from Newfoundland is more than four thousand miles and the voyage usually took four to six weeks, one way. Pernambuco is a state in Brazil and the capital is Recife, a city of half a million people at that time. This was the destination of most of Crosbies' vessels with their cargoes of salt fish. The chief exports of Brazil were sugar, rum and molasses, and that is what the Crosbie ships brought back to Newfoundland. My mother told me that at the time, my father held the record for the quickest trip there and back, but he never talked about it. He was not one to boast. Several years ago I met the well-known politician, Major Peter Cashin, at the home of my

The old homestead in Bay de Verde where my mother grew up and where the wedding reception took place. That's her in the photo with her brother Dan O'Neill.
Photo courtesy Dr. Paul O'Neill

father-in-law Rafe O'Neill and he asked me who my father was. When I told him, he said "Oh yes, Capt. Nicholas Kennedy, he had the record for the quickest round trip to Brazil in a sailing vessel, 45 days." I was glad to have confirmation of my mother's report from such a prominent person. I told Mr. Cashin I was amazed he could remember something that happened so long ago. "Well," he replied, "I can remember that alright, but I can't remember what happened last week." I still doubt the 45 days figure. But what do I know?

While the *Jean* was being discharged in Recife, the newlyweds went shopping. They picked up some trinkets, but one item in particular caught the eye of my mother. It was a fine Persian carpet and she averred how nice it would look back home in their parlor, and it seemed to be just the right size as well. My father looked at the salesclerk and said "Roll it up." The crew were amused as they saw the captain come aboard with a big roll of carpet on his shoulder. The day they were leaving, he bought a huge stalk of very green bananas right there on the pier and carried it aboard. They would soon ripen, he said, and the crew might enjoy the fresh fruit. In a few days they did ripen and the men were invited to help themselves to the bananas hanging in the galley. My mother remembered the last few bananas had to be thrown overboard as they were overripe.

Before arriving back in St. John's, my mother worried about the customs duty they would have to pay on the expensive carpet. "Don't worry," he said, "I'll smuggle it ashore." She laughed and replied, "Oh, sure, you'll put it in your pocket, I suppose." Jumping to his feet he said, "That reminds me. There's something I have to do." With that he took a large canvas sail and spread it out on the deck. Next he took the carpet and rolled it up in the sail so that it now looked like a large roll of canvas. A couple of days after arriving back in port, as a customs officer strolled up and down the pier keeping an eye on all those foreign-going ships, my father nonchalantly put the roll on his shoulder and walked ashore. The customs officer asked him what he had there and he told him he was bringing this sail up the cove to the sailmaker to be repaired and would be bringing it back on board later. The officer let him go, but he had told the truth. He did bring the roll to the sailmaker where he unwrapped the carpet and asked the sailmaker to repair some small rips in the canvas. Of course, he brought the carpet home. My mother was glad having the new carpet but she was still not happy. She thought smuggling was a sin, and even asked a priest about it. The reverend gentleman told her not to worry, There was nothing morally wrong with it. Then she was perfectly happy.

Forty-seven years later, when I left home to be married, that carpet looked nearly as good as new. Of course, when we were growing up we were never allowed in the parlor. That room was reserved for special visitors only, and didn't get much wear.

Capt. Nick fired by Sir John Crosbie

It usually took three or four days to unload a sailing vessel, and the same amount of time to load up with the wooden drums of salt fish. During this time my father lived at home but visited the ship every day to see that the longshoremen were doing things according to plan. One day he surveyed the situation and told the foreman to stop loading. He said putting in any more cargo would overload the ship. The foreman told my father that Sir John had ordered the complete shipment to be put on board, and there were still a lot of drums in the shed. My father argued that he was in charge of this ship and it was up to him how much freight was put aboard. The foreman indignantly replied "Well, you're not my boss, Mr. Crosbie is." "Alright," said my father, "Let's go see him." (Incidentally, Sir. John was the grandfather of renowned politician, John Crosbie.) They both went up to Crosbie's office and explained the problem. Crosbie said he would come down and see what could be done. The three men went to the wharf and boarded the ship. Crosbie observed there was still plenty of space left in the hold, certainly enough for the remaining drums and he told the foreman to put them on board. My father once again warned that to do so would be dangerous. The ship would be overloaded and he would not take her out. Crosbie insisted that this was a complete order and he did not want the customer in Brazil to receive only part of it. My father replied "Then that's it! I will not take that ship out of the harbour." Crosbie was not pleased and told my father that if he would not take the ship out, he would get someone who would. He said "You are discharged." My father made no further comment, just walked away and went home. Later that day an employee of Crosbie and Company who had overheard their conversation, called my father and told him that they put the remainder of the drums on board the ship and she capsized at the wharf.

Crosbie apologized to my father and wanted him back. After all, here was a man who had taken ships tens of thousands of miles on many trips to South America without ever losing a man or a ship, or even touching bottom(running aground). My father would not go back. He would not work for a man who didn't have complete confidence in his qualifications as a Master Mariner.

After leaving Crosbie's, my father signed on with Bowring's, another big exporter, and commanded several steam ships including the *Terra Nova*, which was both a sailing ship and a steamship. Normally steam power was used to drive that ship but if the wind was favorable, sails were unfurled to save fuel. It was during his stint on the Terra Nova that the *S.S. Florizel*, a passenger ship also owned by Bowring's, ran ashore with the loss of ninety-four lives. Forty-four people survived. My father played an important role, together with two other sailors, in rescuing twenty-five people from that ill-fated ship. He would never ask a man to do something he wouldn't do himself and he went along with the two men in a dory from their ship in an attempt to reach the foundering steamer. The seas were so rough they were thrown into the icy water several times but managed to survive. Years later when he developed Creeping Paralysis, some of his friends and even a doctor suggested the disease might have developed as a result of receiving a severe chill during that horrendous rescue operation.

The Wreck of the *Florizel*

The *Florizel* sailed from St. John's Saturday night, Feb. 23, 1918 at 8 p.m., bound for Halifax and New York with 78 passengers and a crew of 60 men. Eight crew members had to remain ashore this trip as they had not been vaccinated and would not be permitted to enter New York. By 10 o'clock a snow storm had developed. Normally on such a voyage, the ship towed a 'log', an instrument shaped like a log of wood that acted as a speedometer. That night there was a lot of slob ice so the device could not be put in the water. Usually at 2 a.m. the ship would be passing Cape Race and changing course to head around the Cape and on to Halifax. With nothing to indicate the ship's speed, and although Capt. Martin had ordered "Full Ahead", he decided to push on for another three hours to make sure they were well below the Avalon Peninsula before changing course to starboard and heading for Halifax.

At 5 a.m. most of the passengers had gone to bed, including the few who had gotten seasick earlier because of the rough seas. From the bridge, the Captain, peering through the blizzard, saw what he thought was a narrow string of ice dead ahead. When he realized he was looking at waves breaking on shore, it was too late. The 3000-ton steamer crashed aground at full speed. The sounds of steel plates hitting rocks and tearing apart were deafening. Many passengers were flung out of their berths and woke up on the floor of their staterooms. Crew members hustled about below deck, knocking on doors and urging passengers to get their lifebelts and go up on deck. Down in the engine room the sea poured in and put out the fires in the boilers. In just a few minutes the steam-driven dynamo failed and the panic-stricken passengers rushing along the passageways, already up to their knees in water, were plunged onto darkness. Some who did manage to climb the companionways and step out on deck were washed overboard to their deaths as huge waves surged over the sinking ship.

When the ship settled, the stern was completely submerged with only the bridge, wireless room and a few feet of the bow still above water. No attempt could be made to launch any of the six lifeboats in such a severe storm, so the crew directed some of the passengers to the relative safety of the bridge and the wireless room. With the coming of daylight, the storm worsened and not only did all the lifeboats break loose from their davits and be lost, but the entire bridge was taken away by another enormous wave, along with the dozens of people who had sought refuge there.

Back in St. John's, my mother awoke to hear someone knocking impatiently at the back door. My father went down and was surprised to see one of the directors of Bowring's who told

S.S. Florizel was a troopship during World War I and brought the "First Five Hundred" overseas.

On the day following the disaster, the *Terra Nova* lies at anchor as crew members in dories remove bodies from the wrecked ship.

him their ship, the *Florizel*, was aground somewhere down the Southern Shore. An S.O.S. had been received, he said, but the signal went dead before the ship could give its location. The director wanted the captain to get the *Terra Nova* underway as quickly as possible and go to the rescue. Several other ships would be going down as well and by the time they were ready to sail, the exact location had been established by residents of the area who saw the tragedy unfold before their eyes but could do nothing to help. It was Cappahayden, 20 miles north of Cape Race.

A call was put out by Bowring's for volunteers to go along and help with the rescue operation. Several Royal Navy seamen came forward and two went along on the *Terra Nova*. The disaster was international news for some time and when my father arrived in New York, now captain of the passenger liner *Prospero*, he was interviewed by several reporters including some from *The Evening Sun* and *The New York Sunday World*. Here is one of their stories:

NEW YORK SUNDAY WORLD   Sunday March 24, 1918

TELLS HOW HEROES SNATCHED 25 FROM DEATH ON FLORIZEL

Canadian Captain and Two
Faced Doom Many Times In Gale-lashed Dory

Capt. Nicholas Kennedy, master of a Canadian sealing steamer that did good work in rescuing passengers from the steamer Florizel, *which was wrecked twenty miles north of Cape Race on Feb. 24, has reached New York.*

To two bluejackets of a British man-of war, who volunteered to go with him, Capt. Kennedy gives most of the credit of the rescue of twenty-five passengers.

It was the bravery and persistence of W. H. Cloute and G. H. Penny, the skipper said, which made it possible to reach the doomed steamer.

"When we reached the Florizel," the Captain said, "the storm was at it's height, and it was impossible to get anywhere near the steamer. A fleet of vessels had gone down from St. John's, and two boats put out from one of the rescue steamers. Both were capsized. Cloute and Penny responded to my call for volunteers to go out in our whaling dory. The best we could do was to pick up the men who had been capsized and return them to their boat. Then we all decided nothing could be done for those on the Florizel."

"A little later when there was a lull in the gale the two men came to me and begged to go out again. So the three of us got into the dory and went at is again. We were capsized five times, but the boat was unsinkable and righted her each time and kept for the stranded steamer."

"The waves were washing over the decks of the steamer, but all through the storm Capt. William Martin remained on deck when it looked impossible to maintain a foothold. We finally got under the lee of the steamer and got twenty-five of the remaining passengers off. A lot of boats were out by this time. Our second dory was launched and she took off eight more men. Other boats succeeded in getting eleven more."

"The last man we got off was Capt. Martin, and there didn't appear to be another soul on board. The storm by this time had increased in violence and our little dory was knocked time and again against the Florizel's side and we thought that every blow was going to smash her to bits. But she survived and did the work cut out for her."

"At that, we didn't get away from the wreck any too soon, for the storm got worse and the Florizel was being battered to pieces by tons of water crashing against her side and waves going *completely over her. I put all we had rescued on the* Prospero *and other craft and ran for Fermuse. Next day we returned to the wreck and picked up seven bodies."*

The final count on that tragedy was 61 passengers lost, together with 33 members of the crew. Afterwards, my father sent a report to the British Admiralty citing the two navy men for bravery, together with seaman H.W. Clouter of the *Terra Nova*, who manned the second dory. The report said in part "I cannot express in words the magnificent heroism, skill and endurance displayed by these three men. The number of lives saved by them is sufficient recommendation." The three were later awarded Medals of Bravery by the Canadian Government.

S.S. Terra Nova, steamship and sailing vessel, was one of the rescue ships at the *Florizel* disaster scene.

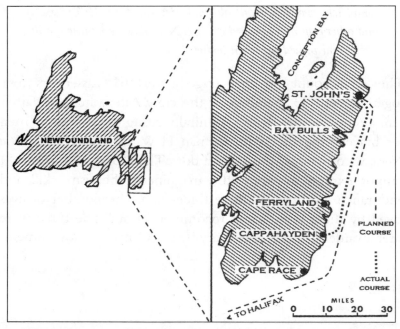

Map shows where passenger ship *Florizel* ran ashore 20 miles north of Cape Race. Ninety-four people died.
Map by Frank Kennedy

Real Reason for Shipwreck

In the late 1940s, the renowned author Cassie Brown was Women's Editor at the *Daily News*, where I worked at the time, and she told me her research led her to believe the engineer on board the *Florizel* had a girlfriend in Halifax and he wanted the ship to arrive late on Tuesday so it would have to stay in that port all night. Cassie claimed he wanted to spend the night with his lady friend and he purposely kept the ship's speed slower than the bridge had ordered. That would explain why the Captain thought he was well past Cape Race when he made the fateful turn. Who knows?

Peter Pan Monument

Many times as children, when visiting Bowring Park, we played around the statue of Peter Pan, sometimes emulating the small bronze figures climbing the base of the monument. One of these little people seemed to be looking at the name "Betty Munn", engraved on a small plaque and probably wondering, as we were, "Who is this person?" Another engraving proclaimed, "In memory of a little girl who loved the Park." Could this be the same young lady? It certainly was and my dad told me Betty Munn was a little girl lost in the *Florizel* disaster. Betty and her father, John S. Munn, had boarded the passenger ship to go to New York where Mrs. Munn was being treated in hospital. Mr. Munn also lost his life and the child's god-father, Sir Edgar Bowring, was so upset with the loss of this child he so dearly loved, that he wanted a permanent memorial erected in her memory, and placed in the park that he had donated to the city a few years earlier.

Sir Edgar commissioned the famous English sculptor, Sir George Frampton, to duplicate a monument he had created for a public garden in London. Sir George not only made the monument, he sailed across the ocean with it and picked a location in Bowring Park to have it displayed. The Peter Pan monument was put in place near the boat pool and unveiled in August, 1925. Sir George declared that this setting was even more beautiful than the location of the original statue in London.

The Peter Pan statue in Bowring Park was erected by Sir Edgar Bowring in August 1925 in memory of his young godchild, Betty Munn, who died in the *Florizel* disaster in 1918.
Photo by Frank Kennedy

Eugene's Most Embarrassing Moment

In the mid 1920s the *S.S. Sagona*, with my father as Captain, was chartered to bring pit props from Botwood to Bell Island. Pit props are large wooden logs were used to shore up the iron mines which were in full production at that time. The ship made several trips that year and during the summer, my father took my brother, Eugene, then a young teenager, along with him. Eugene told me later that sometimes there was dense fog in Conception Bay and while radar had not yet been invented, our dad used the same principle to locate the island. Eugene thought it was a pretty slick trick and something he probably didn't learn in navigation school.

After passing Baccalieu Island and steaming several miles into the bay, the Captain would sound the ship's horn and listen for the echo. The cliffs of Bell Island are two to three hundred feet high and perpendicular, running straight down into the sea. When the sound hit the cliff and the echo returned, the Captain steered the ship in the direction of the echo, gradually slowing the vessel as the timing of the echo-return decreased. Eventually eye contact was made and there was no danger of running aground as there was deep water right up to the base of the cliff. By steaming along parallel to the island, the pier was easily located.

On one trip from Botwood, my father realized he could not get back to Bell Island and have Eugene back in St. John's in time for the school opening in early September. He decided to send him back by train, so he took the *Sagona* in to a port along the way, probably Gambo or Glovertown, where the railway ran close to the public wharf. With the steamer safely tied up, my father took Eugene and his small suitcase and walked the short distance to the railway station. It so happened he knew the station-master and inquired about the train to St. John's. It would be along in a couple of hours, he was told. My father bought a ticket and asked the station-master to keep an eye on Eugene and be sure to put him aboard when the train arrived. Knowing his son was in good hands, my father walked back to the ship and sailed away.

Florence Kennedy holds what are probably the first two shells fired by Newfoundland in World War I. They were fired from the British Naval Ship *Petrel*. Ms. Kennedy's grandfather, Capt. Nick Kennedy, was a lieutenant in the Royal Naval Reserve and Captain of the *Petrel* at the time.
Photo by Frank Kennedy

The train arrived on time and Eugene got aboard with his suitcase and sat down opposite two well-dressed men who were both reading magazines. As the train pulled away, one of the men looked up and asked Eugene, "What station was that we just left?" "I don't know, sir." replied my brother. "But you just got on there, didn't you?" insisted the man. "Yes sir." answered Eugene. Then the other man got into the act with, "You just got on at that last station and you don't know the name of it?" "No sir." said Eugene. The two men looked at each other, rolled their eyes upwards and resumed reading their magazines. In a short while the conductor came through the car and one of the men inquired about the station they had just passed. When they were told, one of them looked at Eugene and remarked, "Did you hear that, Stupid?" Eugene spent the rest of the journey looking out the window. He was a very shy teenager, too shy to explain how he got to the station. And anyway, who would believe him if he said his father just dropped him off by steamer. Oh sure! A likely story. It must have been very embarrassing for a clever young guy who, as I mentioned earlier, always came first in his class in school.

A Last Word About the Skipper

Early in World War I he was attached to the coastal patrol of Newfoundland as a lieutenant in the Royal Navy Reserve and was appointed Captain of *H.M.S. Petrel*. That ship's mandate was to watch for enemy submarines or ships along the east coast of the island. One day a ship was sighted with no flag flying. The *Petrel* signaled that ship to identify it's nationality by raising it's colors. When several requests went unanswered and the ship continued on its course, the Captain ordered two rounds fired across the ship's bow. The 60mm cannon was put into action and two shells went whistling across the bow of the steamer. The crew of the *Petrel* were amused at how quickly a Union Jack was raised to the masthead. It was a British ship, of course, so no further action was taken.

My father believed these were the first two shells fired by Newfoundland in World War I, and he was probably right, so he saved the shell casings and brought them home as souvenirs. I still have them in my possession. They are solid brass, 14.5 inches long and 2.5 inches in diameter at the base. I suppose they should be handed over to a museum. The only problem is that I have no documentation to prove their history except my father's word, which I certainly believe, but I feel any curator would want more proof of their authenticity. Any takers? Contact me at **kennedykamera@rogers.nl.ca**

chapter 14

BIG BUSINESS AND THE NORTHERN LIGHTS

· FIRST CHARGE ACCOUNT ·

At the age of 14, I opened my first ever charge account at Mr. Pat Piccott's candy store in the next block at the corner of Pleasant and Carnell Streets. Mr. Piccott, a kind and gracious gentleman, usually tended the store himself. Occasionally, his lovely daughter, Kitty, would pinch-hit for him and it was very nice to drop in, sometimes without any cash on hand, especially if she was there, and buy a crinkle or raisin square for three cents and a bottle of root or birch beer for five cents, or four banner caramels for two cents or a jaw-breaker for one cent. I don't remember how the arrangement got started, but Mr. Piccott jotted down the purchase in a little notebook and I paid off the account at the end of each week. He put no credit limit on my purchases but I never allowed myself to go over fifty cents for the week. Of course, I'm sure my parents would not be happy if they knew what was going on but they never found out. Perhaps if I ran up a bill that I couldn't handle, they would have been made aware of it, but that didn't happen and I enjoyed being trusted by Mr. Piccott.

There were five small candy stores in our neighborhood and hundreds around the city. Usually the front room or parlor of a house was converted to a small shop. Most had a bell attached to the inside of the door to alert the owner when a customer entered. Just across the street there was Mr. Charlie Roud's store. His brother, William, whom I mentioned in Chapter Three as being the most popular man in St. John's, also owned a candy store at the top of Power Street. He, too, had a lovely daughter, Catherine, who sometimes served in the store. It seems most of the shopkeepers in our neighborhood had lovely daughters. Remember Joan Duffy whom I mentioned earlier? On Pleasant Street there were three stores within two blocks, not counting Duffy's: Vavasour's, Waddens, and of course, Piccott's. No one made a living from these little shops. They were just a means of earning some extra cash to supplement regular incomes in the lean years during the Depression. None of the shops had refrigerators, but Roud's on Power Street, unlike the others, had an icebox which made very nice cold soft drinks available on warm summer days.

Over the years as the proprietors passed away and their children went on to other endeavors, these five little stores and dozens of similar shops around town closed down. Larger shops began appearing, referred to as 'Groc and Conf stores'. This was a contraction of Grocery and Confectionery store, and were later renamed Convenience Stores.

In 1936 the Government, with lobbying from city store clerks, passed a Shop Act requiring all department stores and large grocery outlets to remain closed on Sundays, after 6:30 p.m. weekdays, and after 12:30 p.m. Wednesdays. So there was what was called a 'half holiday' in the middle of the week.

This was a great boost for the convenience stores, since they were permitted to remain open all night if they so desired, and they carried a variety of grocery items. After a few weeks the larger grocery stores, not yet called supermarkets, such as Ayres, Bowring's and others complained to government that the Shop Act was unfair to them and the scores of Groc. & Conf. stores were taking away business from them. The government came up with a compromise. The act was amended to state that no store could sell or display any items that were considered groceries after hours. That satisfied the 'big boys,' but the small store owners got around the 'display' part of the act by moving all their groceries to the rear of their shops and drawing a curtain across when closing time came. The candies, chocolate bars, soft drinks and fruit etc. were all in the front section and so the groceries were 'not displayed.' Of course if a customer wanted a tin of beans or a pound of Solo butter, the owner went behind the curtain and fetched the item. The government knew about this and sometimes sent 'spies' out to watch for infringements. Some retailers were taken to court and fined. My wife, Ruth, told me she remembers when she was growing up on Bond Street, sometimes at night, her mother would send her to the store next door for a can of peas or a tin of fruit and she was warned that if there was another customer in the store, not to ask for the item. "Just buy some candy," she was told, "and go back later."

Three years later World War II broke out and the government, and everyone else for that matter, had more to worry about that the odd can of soup being sold illegally and the enforcement of the Shop Act was discontinued.

The Northern Lights

In the 1920s and '30s, with so many hills in St. John's, sliding was a very popular winter sport for children. It was not permitted on all city streets, however, but city council had enacted a law designating certain streets where it was allowed. The street closest to our home was only a block away, Power Street. That street was fairly steep and ideal for sliding and we spent a lot of time there. In the early days there were no motor cars and we went down over that street dozens of times in an afternoon after school. Some of our friends had a homemade bobsled where two sleds were connected with a long plank. Half a dozen kids could ride on that one.

I remember one day in particular when conditions were perfect, no cars, no horses, no wind, not too cold but cold enough to keep the snow from melting and a nice fast run down the hill every time. I was enjoying it so much that even after my friends went home for supper, I kept at it. My mother had told me to come home as soon as it got dark, but I was having such great fun that I determined I was not quitting sliding for a while yet. Although it was quite dark now, there was a dim street light at the bottom of the hill, so I could still see what I was doing. Suddenly, as I walked back up Power Street pulling my sled, I saw this weird huge green light flashing across the sky. I was terrified. In all my seven years on earth I had never seen anything like this. My frightened little mind came up with the idea that it must be the Almighty, about to wreak vengeance on me for disobeying my mother. Maybe I was about to be struck by lightning or some similar horrible fate. I was afraid to look at the sky anymore and ran home with my head down, looking only at the snow in front of my feet. Of course it was the Northern Lights, Aurora Borealis, but I'd never even heard of that before. When I arrived home I was totally surprised that my mother didn't seem upset with my tardiness. Instead, she asked "Are you all right, Frank? You look pale." I told her I was okay, just a bit cold. I was so relieved that she was not angry with me and I figured that if she was not displeased then maybe God was not offended either, and perhaps I wouldn't go to Hell after all. I never forgot that day, nor how scared I was.

It was much later that I found out I was seeing a natural phenomenon that has been described as a long wavy band or curtain of colored light high in the sky, predominantly green, often with shades of yellow and occasionally red. Sometimes it appears in the form of huge flashes traveling across the sky, as with my first encounter. The Aurora is rarely seen in the southern United States or southern Europe. Back in the dark ages the Romans and Greeks viewed these displays with superstition and as omens of coming calamities. The Northern Lights are thought to have some connection with the earth's magnetism and the occurrence of sun spots. Nowadays they are rarely observed over bright cities, and even in smaller towns, the street lighting diminishes the odds of seeing the beautiful spectacle. There have been measurements showing their height above the earth as an amazing 60 to 100 miles. The wonderful lights are also visible in the southern hemisphere where they are known as "Southern Lights," or Aurora Australis.

We were warned by our parents that if a policeman saw us sliding on our own street we would be put in jail, so we rarely did slide on Patrick or Pleasant Streets. One day when we were doing just that I saw another boy ahead of me jump off his sled and run away when he spotted a policeman on the beat. I don't know what happened to his sled, as I jumped off mine as well and ran home pulling it with me. I saw another boy actually run into the legs of a horse. The animal hardly moved, but again the boy jumped off and ran away, abandoning his sled.

Eating Out

Sometimes on a cold winter day, after school, my friend Jack Browne and I walked down to a Chinese restaurant on Water Street just west of Patrick Street and had a nice bowl of hot soup for five cents. Our mothers didn't know about that either. They wouldn't appreciate it. On other occasions we bought a tray of chips (french fries) for the same price at Stacey's Fish & Chips van if it was in our neighborhood. Fish and chips were available starting at ten cents. This one-of-a-kind truck was usually parked near the CLB Armory on Harvey Road, but Mr. Stacey often parked in various locations around town and set up for a few hours. Sometimes he parked at the top of Patrick Street in front of St. Clare's Hospital and that is where we patronized him. The deep fryer was heated by a coal stove with a smoke stack on the roof. When the stove was being stoked there was a lot of smoke from the funnel and sometimes neighbors complained, so the very obliging Mr. Stacey would move to another location. If there was a partic-ularly good picture playing at one of the local movie theaters, you could depend on Stacey's van being parked near the line-up and doing a brisk business. The most profitable day for that man must have been Regatta Day when the van was parked near Quidi Vidi lake for the entire day. Of course at the Regatta he had competition, but not a lot. There were many hot-dog stands, but all that was needed there was boiling water to heat the wieners. Portable deep fryers were scarce.

What was popular at the races back then was hop beer, and there were hop beer tents all over the place selling it for five cents a mug. Unlike modern times, it would not be unusual to see five or six drunks passed out on the shores of the lake. I remember one day seeing a drunk lying near the boathouse with his fly open. A policeman just happened to be passing by and had the gall to ask me if I would button it up. (No zippers back then.) I didn't even answer him but walked away in disgust. There was no law against selling beer to an intoxicated person, and a lot of that was done while the customer could still stand at the tent. Sometimes the inebriates became abusive and were arrested on the spot. The police van or 'Black Maria,' as it was called, stood by at the lakeside and made several trips to the lockup in the course of the day, and by the time the last race was run, perhaps a dozen or more were sleeping it off in the cells. None of these were ever charged, however, unless they had caused damage or assaulted someone, and as they gradually attained a state of sobriety, they were free to go home.

I still remember my first visit to a soda fountain. I was taken there by my older brother, Jack. At that time he worked in the engine room of the passenger liner, S.S. Sylvia, which made regular trips to New York. The ship was in port a few days every month and one day my brother told me to come down and he would show me around the ocean liner. He told me that when I came aboard I should ask for, "Jack Kennedy, Oh yeah." He explained that there were two Jack Kennedys working on board and it seems, "Oh yeah," was an expression often used by him. It certainly worked, for when I went on board the ship which was moored at Harvey's pier and asked for Jack Kennedy, one of the crew asked "Which one?" When I said "Oh yeah!" I was taken directly to my brother.

He gave me a tour of the ship and decided to walk home with me. On the way home along Water Street we stopped at a Soda Fountain. I don't remember the name, but it was near the Queen Theater and we sat on high stools and I enjoyed my first malted milk. That made my day. There were only three or four soda fountains in the city seventy-five years ago, and I remember this one.

My father had four sons but no one followed in his footsteps of going to sea to make a living except Jack. And even he gave it up after a couple of years and went to work in the mines at Buchans. Although these mines were well known for their output of lead, zinc and copper, Jack told me a fair amount of gold came out of the mines there as well, but the miners were warned by the company not to mention this to any outsiders. He thought the company would have to pay extra royalties if the government was aware of the gold finds. When Jack left Buchans, he brought back his miner's hat, complete with lamp, and gave it to me. That was a real treasure. The lamp attached to the front of the hard hat was a carbide lamp. It was shaped much like a can of pop with the top half containing water and the bottom filled with calcium carbide, a gray powder. When water contacts this chemical, a very inflammable gas, acetylene, is formed. Inside the lamp, the water is allowed to leak slowly into the lower section and the gas formed is channeled to a small opening at the front of the lamp and when ignited forms a steady white flame which lasts several hours. These, of course, were used in the early days of mining before small electric lights with batteries came on the market.

chapter 15

WARTIME
IN ST. JOHN'S

Prisoners of War Held in City

Two days after World War II broke out in 1939, the first German prisoners of war were locked up in St. John's. Downtown shoppers were amazed to see the twenty-five men marching along Water Street under heavy guard. Citizens of the Capital City realized the war had indeed begun.

Britain and France declared war on Germany on Sept. 3, after that country invaded Poland. Although Canada did not enter the war until a week later, this was before Confederation. Newfoundland was a British colony, and as such became involved in the conflict immediately. At Botwood a German merchant ship, the *S.S. Christoph Doornum*, which was loading newsprint, was seized and its crew were made prisoners of war. They were brought to St. John's by train and marched from the railway station to the Y.M.C.A. building on Water Street east. There they were imprisoned during the construction of a proper internment camp at Pleasantville (later to become Fort

Pepperell). When they were transferred to the new camp, they met some of their fellow countrymen who were unlucky enough to be on board a ship loading iron ore at Bell Island on Sept. 3. After some months all these POWs were moved to a larger facility in Western Canada. At the time nothing was published in the media about these foreigners, but the news got around by word of mouth. Citizens often strolled along the Boulevard on a Sunday afternoon to sneak a peep at "the enemy". For the next few weeks life went on pretty much as usual in St. John's.

Call for Volunteers

On Feb. 6, Governor Walwyn issued a proclamation asking for volunteers to serve in the British Army for the duration of the war. He wanted 400 recruits and within days that number was reached as patriotic young men, the majority from St. John's, came forward to serve their country. In succeeding months hundreds also joined the Royal Navy and the Royal Air Force.

In Europe during the first year of the conflict things went badly for Great Britain. Not only had Germany invaded Holland and Belgium, but the unbelievable happened: France was overcome by the enemy. Scores of German submarines were patrolling the waters off the British Isles and sinking dozens of merchant supply ships every week, cutting off badly needed war materials. In August, 1940, Germany began bombing London. England was being driven to its knees.

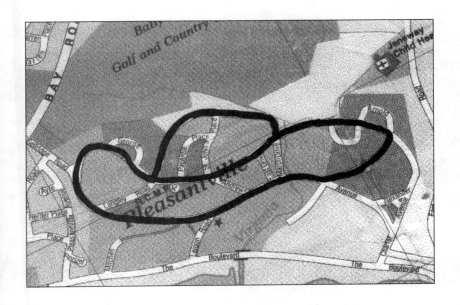

Lt. Col. Phillip Burton, a Texas urban planner, came to Newfoundland and designed Fort Pepperell. Wanting to leave his mark, he designed the road system in the shape of a ten-gallon hat.
Photo courtesy CBC Archives

Churchill Asks for Help

British Prime Minister Sir Winston Churchill appealed to his old friend, Franklin D. Roosevelt, President of the United States, for assistance against the German forces. Roosevelt realized that if Britain was invaded, the next conquest for Hitler would be North America. The stepping stone to that continent was obviously the island of Newfoundland, the nearest territory to Europe, and America was determined to defend that island against possible aggression. And so the famous Lend-Lease Agreement was born, and it would have a tremendous effect on the financial and social life of Newfoundland and especially St. John's.

The Lend-Lease Agreement

The United States agreed to supply fifty warships (destroyers) to Britain in exchange for a 99-year lease on territories in Newfoundland, Bermuda and the West Indies. The areas would be used as military defense bases. U.S. engineers carried out land, sea and air surveys of virtually all the east coast of the island and Labrador to decide where the bases should be built. A delegation under the command of U.S. Rear Admiral Greenslade met with the Commission of Government to discuss their plans. Bases would be set up in Goose Bay, Argentia, Stephenville and St. John's. The largest was to be located at Pleasantville in St. John's and take in more than 200 acres that was mostly farm land, with a few summer houses. Pleasantville was the site where 26 years earlier, the famous "First Five Hundred" young Newfoundland soldiers trained before going overseas to serve in World War I. The new base would be called Fort Pepperell in memory of a famous 18th century U.S. military leader, Sir William Pepperell. The boundary to the south would be Quidi Vidi Lake and to the north, Bally Haly Golf and Curling Club on Logy Bay Road. All property owners were notified their land was urgently required for the defense of the country, and they were duly compensated by the U.S. Government and asked to move out as quickly as possible.

Fort Pepperell, Threat to the Annual Regatta

For security reasons, the plans for the establishment of a military base at Pleasantville were never published. However, when Mayor Andy Carnell, the city councilors, and the Regatta committee discovered the plans included taking over all the north bank of Quidi Vidi lake, right to the water's edge, they were up in arms. This action would mean the end of the oldest continuing sporting event in North America, the annual St. John's Regatta, which began more than 120 years earlier. Or at least it would have to be postponed for 99 years. The land in question ran the full length of the lake between the Boulevard and the high water mark of the lake. Just recently the city had designated this whole area as "The King George V Memorial Park" and Mayor Carnell expressed the hope that some day they would build a stadium near the head of the lake. Members of the Commission of Government contacted the U.S. authorities and they agreed to change the south boundary to exclude the Boulevard and the north bank. Instead, the Boulevard would be rebuilt, along with King's Bridge Road, which was the principal route from St. John's harbour to the new base.

Paving the Way

On a rainy day in October, 1941, a small naval boat came in to the wharf at Bursey's Fish Plant on the south side of St. John's harbour. Several naval officers stepped ashore and asked to see the owner. Mr. W.J. Bursey was surprised to see four men, decorated with gold braid, enter his office at the rear of the plant. He was astounded when, after introducing themselves as U.S. Naval officers, he was told they wanted to rent his premises and hoped he could move out the following day. They told Mr. Bursey that in the interest of the defense of Newfoundland it was essential to have his property. There was a troopship in New York ready to sail for St. John's and his dock was the only place in the entire harbour where the water was deep enough for that ship to moor. Before answering the question regarding moving out the next day, Mr. Bursey said "Gentlemen, let me show you around." Bursey took the visitors to a shed where 1000 quintals (12,000 lbs.) of salt fish were stored, as well as another 12,000 lbs of pickled fish in vats waiting to be put into casks. In the cod oil factory he showed them 10,000 gallons of cod liver oil that were 'curing' in tanks and barrels. Outside on the wharf, men were gutting fish and extracting the livers. The Americans were very impressed with the scope of Bursey's operation and realized moving out quickly would be impossible. They showed Bursey a drawing of the troopship *Edmund B. Alexander* tied up at his premises. In a few days an agreement was signed and Mr. Bursey was very happy with the arrangement. Not only was he paid a generous price for the rental, but he would be allowed to continue with his business and the Americans agreed to have him supply provisions for the ship during the eight months it would be in port.

The *Edmund B. Alexander*

On January 29, 1941, the largest ship ever to enter St. John's harbour to that date passed through The Narrows with only two feet of water between the keel and the bottom. It was the

22,600 ton U.S. Troopship *Edmund B. Alexander*, nearly 700 feet long. Although it was wartime, America was not yet involved, and although the ship was not mentioned by the media, everyone knew the ship would arrive, as she had been "hanging around" for four days before entering the harbour. The ship was a prize of World War I, having been in Boston when that war broke out; it was then a German passenger ship, the *S.S. Amerika*. It was renamed to honor a great U.S. Commander who served in the Mexican war 1846–48.

When the troopship left New York on Jan. 15, none of the 977 military men on board or the 200 crew members had any idea where they were headed, except, of course, a few officers. All they knew was "they were going overseas". Five days later, during a snowstorm, the ship dropped anchor one mile off St. John's harbour. The Customs boat *Shulamite* went out to meet her. On board were Captain John Whelan and U.S. Capt. Hiatt, as well as harbour pilot Capt. George Anstey, who would later guide the ship through The Narrows. What they saw as they emerged from a snow squall was startling: a huge gray wall with hundreds of portholes towering above them. It was the port side of the ship. After some discussion the ship's Captain William Joensen and the pilot, Capt. Anstey, decided it would be risky to try bringing this large ship through the Narrows in such rough seas and as the forecast showed no immediate improvement in the bad weather, the *Edmund B.* would weigh anchor and steam to Conception Bay to await better conditions.

The ship lay at anchor for three days between Bell Island and Kelly's Island and was admired by thousands all along Conception Bay South, as well as hundreds of St. John's residents who went out to Topsail to see the big visitor. Very early on Wednesday, January 29, the *Edmund B.* sailed out of

Conception Bay and was soon at anchor once more outside the Narrows. Again the *Shulamite* went out to meet her. As they approached, Capt. Anstey and the others were impressed with the large ocean liner. Her five decks, four tall masts and two funnels gave an impression of incredible height. As the customs boat came near 'the great gray wall,' two metal doors swung open in the side of the ship and Capt. Anstey climbed in and was escorted to the bridge. There he met the ship's Captain, William Joensen, for the first time. Once again the anchor was winched up and the two men guided the ship safely through the channel as hundreds watched from Signal Hill, the Battery and Fort Amherst.

The U.S. troopship *Edmund B. Alexander* remained 8 months at Bursey's Fish premises on the Southside in 1941. It was the only pier in the harbor where the water was deep enough for the ship to moor.
Photo by Frank Kennedy

When the ship was securely moored at Bursey's premises, the same metal doors swung open again and a long gangway was pushed out to the wharf. Hundreds of soldiers who had been at sea for two weeks began streaming ashore and setting foot on this new found land for the first time. As they poured into the city they were delighted to see U.S. flags flying, and on Water Street many of the mercantile firms were decorated with bunting. "The friendly invasion", as it was so aptly called in John Cardoulis' book of that name, had begun. Capitulation was inevitable. Fraternization was rampant. Surrender was bounteous. By the year 1990, 25,000 Newfoundland women would have married American servicemen. Of course, thousands of these servicemen were stationed in other areas of Newfoundland and Labrador but here we are writing only about the effect of the war on St. John's.

Heavy Artillery

Bursey's fish plant workers were amazed to see twelve war tanks come off the ship, as well as many anti-aircraft guns and several large cannon. The ship had carried, as well as the troops, 2000 tons of war materials and building supplies. The latter were taken to Pleasantville and the following month construction of Fort Pepperell commenced. This would be the largest U.S. base outside America. The cannon were immediately put in place on Signal Hill, at Fort Amherst and other points along the coast to guard against any possible attack from the ocean. An anti-aircraft artillery unit was set up just below Cabot Tower in the location now occupied by the Interpretation Center and was manned 24 hours a day.

Floating Barracks

For the remainder of the winter the *Edmund B.* was used as a barracks to house the soldiers. During that time many fishermen from the Battery and Fort Amherst ran an unofficial ferry service back and forth, using their fishing boats, from the ship to the north side of the harbour. In May the troops were moved to a temporary camp near Carpasian Road, named Camp Alexander, to await the construction of permanent buildings at the new base. In Camp Alexander the living conditions under canvas were a giant step down from the comforts of the *Edmund B.* which had all the conveniences of a passenger liner including large dining halls, a movie theater, a swimming pool and a hospital.

Economic Boom for St. John's

The construction of the base was a great boost to the economy of St. John's and indeed the whole island, for workers came from all across the country to work there. In the summer of 1941 more than 5000 civilians were employed, and even after that work was finished, more that 2000 civilians found employment there for several years. Earlier that same year, several residents of the Lower Battery got their marching orders and their homes were torn down to make room for a U.S. Army dock and two huge storage sheds. Hundreds were employed on that job as well and it cost the U.S. government nearly two million dollars.

With construction at Pepperell almost complete by November 1941, troops began moving in from Camp Alexander. Now they found they were housed in the most modern accommodations ever built for the military outside the U.S. To add to that opulence, all the married officers were allowed to bring in their wives and families from the States. That luxury didn't last long, however, as on December 7, after Pearl Harbour was bombed, the order was sent out to have all the civilians move out, except workers, to make room for additional troops. Troopships kept arriving and by 1942 there were 7000 military personnel at Fort Pepperell.

Social Life

The influx of thousands of soldiers on 24-hour passes from Fort Pepperell resulted in a great increase in night life activity in St. John's. The U.S.O. building (United Services Organization) on Merrymeeting Road, The Red Triangle Hostel (Y.M.C.A) on Water Street west and the K. of C. Hostel (Knights of Columbus) on Harvey Road, were well patronized. This was before the coming of television so the nine movie theaters were also well attended. Add to that the hundreds of Canadian Army and Navy servicemen stationed in the area and there was no shortage of escorts for the single ladies of the city. My older sister, Mary, worked as a volunteer hostess at the U.S.O. and every night after work a different serviceman walked her home in the blackout. They never got inside the house, though, my mother saw to that. Before the war Mary worked for a few years at Long Brothers Printers, but when my father became bedridden she quit her job and remained home helping our mother looking after him over the years. She was a wonderful, kind lady and didn't marry until after he died, and then to a civilian, John McCormack, from St. Joseph's, Salmonier, a member of the National Convention.

There seemed to be more sailors in our area of town than soldiers, no doubt due to the R.C.N station in nearby Buckmaster's Field. I remember the time our dog Mac went missing for four days. When he finally turned up he seemed well fed and none the worse for being AWOL. However, ever after that, whenever he saw a sailor walking by our house, he would bark furiously until that man was out of sight. We figured Mac was probably kidnapped by a sailor and taken to the barracks but managed to get away and find his way home. And speaking of sailors, I remember one day I was helping my brother, Eugene, take down blackout shutters from his store on Water Street just opposite the railway turntable pit. This was where the locomotives were turned around for a trip back across the island. We both had our backs to the pit, only a hundred feet behind us, when we heard this rapid, Chug! Chug! Chug!, the sound of a steam engine going full speed. Before we could turn around there was a tremendous "bam" as the eighty-ton locomotive plunged eight feet into the pit. The ground shook violently as if an earthquake was in progress. Looking around we saw a man in a sailor suit in the cab struggling with the controls and then the four driving wheels ran rapidly in reverse. The front of the engine was buried in the ground and the locomotive had stopped at a 45 degree angle with the wheels now suspended in midair. That behemoth was going nowhere and neither was the driver, at the moment. It was a drunken sailor and with some fumbling around, he managed to shut off the engine and stagger out into the arms of the railway police. They held him until the arrival of a navy paddy wagon and we never saw him after that.

Newfoundland Attacked by German U-Boats

On a quiet, cool afternoon in March, 1942, residents of the city were startled at the sound of 500 lbs. of dynamite exploding in the Narrows. "They must be blasting away some rocks to make the entrance to the harbour deeper," suggested one observer in the east end of the city. Looking towards the narrows he saw a cloud of black smoke rising from the sea near Fort Amherst

Two minutes later there was a flash of orange flame and a great plume of water and rocks went skyward near the Outer Battery. Two German torpedoes had exploded in the Narrows. A submarine just outside the harbour had attempted to sink a large merchant ship at anchor awaiting a convoy. Fortunately the commander's aim was not good and the missiles hit both sides of the narrows with no serious damage. Immediately the alarm was sounded and guns were manned at Fort Amherst and on Signal Hill. Spotters were at their action stations but there was no sign of the enemy and nothing to shoot at. The sub had made a clean getaway.

The Bell Island Attack

Six months later and 14 miles due west of the Narrows, on Sept. 5, 1942, it was a different story when two 'ore boats' were sunk in Conception Bay near Bell Island with the loss of 29 lives. In November two more ships were torpedoed in the same location and 40 men died. In the first incident, two steamships already loaded with iron ore were at anchor off Bell Island's Lance Cove waiting to join a convoy, and their captains were attending a secret meeting in St. John's making arrangements to meet that convoy. The first victim was the *S.S. Saganaga*, with 8800 tons of ore in her holds. She went to the bottom in less than a minute, taking 29 crew members with her. There had been no sign of trouble until a torpedo exploded amidships and another a few seconds later finished the job. It was just after 11:00 a.m. on a calm, overcast day. The chief engineer of the nearby *Lord Strathcona*, now in charge in the absence of the captain and realizing they were "sitting ducks," gave the order to man the lifeboats and abandon ship, not only to save themselves but to rescue some of the survivors of the *Saganaga* who were swimming around amongst the wreckage.

As they were preparing to launch the lifeboats they heard and felt a bump. Something had hit the bottom of their ship. They thought it might be a torpedo that failed to explode. There was no panic. The men carried out their duties just as they had often done in practice runs, but this time as they were rowing away from the ship there was a tremendous explosion behind them and their ship disappeared in less than two minutes. When a ship is loaded with iron ore, and a hole as big as a house is blown in the side of the ship, the rush of water sends that ship to the bottom very quickly, quicker than a ship with any other cargo. All the crew of the *Lord Strathcona* escaped injury, due certainly in part to a miscalculation on the part of the commander of the sub that did the sinking.

Submarine's Log

The log of that submarine, the *U-513*, made public after the war, shows that shortly after sinking the first ship, the commander decided to come up and look around. He was not aware that he was now directly underneath the second ship and as the sub began rising it hit the keel of that ship. He knew the bump would be felt on board the ship and expecting depth charges to be dropped, let the sub sink to the bottom of the bay in 150 feet of water. He was relieved to find the bottom in that location was soft, not rocky as his charts indicated. In the state of panic the sub had hit hard. After twenty anxious minutes, expecting the worst, there was a slight leak but no sound of depth charges and the sub quietly moved ahead and came up to periscope level. Then with the *Lord Strathcona* lined up in the crosshairs, two torpedoes were fired and both found their mark. The ship sank in one and a half minutes with not a soul on board.

Periscope Sighted

The periscope was sighted by other ships in the area and the Mercantile Navy men on board went into action. First off the mark was the *S.S. Rose Castle*, a coal boat at the Scotia Pier. She came out with guns blazing. Four-inch shells were exploding in the water all around the periscope, which quickly disappeared as the sub beat a hasty retreat. Many shells ricocheted off the calm water and landed in Beachy Cove, St. Phillip's and Broad Cove. People living there thought they were being attacked but fortunately no one was hurt. A rumor circulated that the Home Defense guns on the island were meant to guard against air attacks and could not be aimed down to the sea from their 300 foot high location and their shells were going straight across the bay. This was not so. These guns also fired shells at the last sighted location of the periscope and in fact, several unexploded shells picked up in the above-mentioned settlements were turned over to the authorities and were found not to match the type fired from the island.

Spreading the News

Word of these attacks spread like wildfire throughout St. John's and it was reported next day that there were German Submarines trapped in Conception Bay and being hunted down by warships. That day being Sunday, hundreds of curious people went to Topsail and Portugal Cove to view the activity. We went to Topsail and there were two small warships cruising up and down the bay and at one point a bomber flew low over the water. Many spectators hoped to see bombs dropping but that did not happen as the sub was long gone. Actually, shortly after the sinking the previous day, the captain of the Bell Island ferry reported seeing the swirling of a sub passing along under water on its way out the bay. The log of that U-boat also shows that before the two ships were sunk, two torpedoes were launched but failed to make contact. The Commander wrote they sank to the bottom. That would mean that to this very day there are two torpedoes rusting away somewhere out there, each containing 500 lbs. of dynamite. Monday's newspapers carried only this very vague item regarding the tragedy:

> *"It was announced by the Naval Authorities yesterday that a submarine attack was made in Newfoundland coastal waters. Further details of the accident have not been released."*

Second Attack

Two months later the Germans were back. A different submarine this time, but with the same deadly mission. It was the *U-518* on its maiden voyage from Germany and it picked Newfoundland as the first stop. Late at night on Nov. 2, residents of the Front on Bell Island were awakened by an explosion that shook them in their beds. They knew what it had to be. Another torpedo. This time the Scotia Pier was blown apart by a torpedo intended for the *S.S. Anna A*, tied up there to unload coal. In the darkness, the sub commander, not realizing he had missed his target, lined up an ore carrier, the *S.S. Rose Castle*. That ship had narrowly escaped being sunk in September during the first attack and had actually fired at the U-boat, but this time her luck ran out and she went to the bottom with a loss of 28 lives, including several Newfoundlanders one of whom was from St. Johns, a Mr. H. King. By now the bay was lit up with flares fired from the island by the Home Defense. The U-boat quickly submerged, but before so doing fired one last torpedo at the 6000 ton Free French ship *PLM 26*, which being already loaded with ore, went down in a few seconds with twelve of the fifty crew members. Searchlights on the island kept scanning the waters in the immediate area but that sub was not seen until well after daylight when a patrol bomber sighted it near Cape Race heading out to sea. A bombing attack was immediately initiated but before that could be accomplished, the infamous Newfoundland fog moved in and the sub escaped once more.

That U-boat continued its mission of destruction for more than two years until April 22, 1945, just three weeks before the war ended, when it was sent to the bottom of the Atlantic with all hands near the Azores by a U.S. Destroyer. At that time, however, the commander who was responsible for the tragedies in Conception Bay had already been retired and was replaced by another ill-fated officer.

The Sinking of the *Caribou*

Another wartime disaster I well remember is the sinking of the ferry *Caribou* and the shocking loss of innocent lives. It's very disheartening to realize that when the *S.S. Caribou* was hit by a German torpedo, that ship was actually a legitimate target, according to the universal rules of war. The *Caribou* was carrying military troops. Notwithstanding, it seems a very cruel act considering the 137 men, women and children who were killed in that disaster. The log of the submarine showed the Germans thought they were attacking a freighter being accompanied by a warship, not that that would have made much difference.

The 2200 ton passenger ferry sailed from North Sydney, Nova Scotia, at 8:00 p.m. on Oct. 13 for an overnight crossing to Port-aux-Basques with 45 crew members and 206 passengers, including 99 servicemen. Some were Royal Air Force men who had just completed training and were coming back to the island on leave before going overseas. Others were army and navy personnel on various assignments. The ship was overcrowded and there were not enough berths for all the women and children. Some servicemen gave up their berths to lady passengers and sat up in the lounge for the night, and that act of generosity was responsible for saving many of their lives.

The *Caribou* was equipped with six lifeboats and four life rafts and before leaving port, all passengers were assigned certain lifeboat stations in case of emergency. However, on that particular night, no lifeboat drill was carried out. By midnight most of the passengers had retired in anticipation of an early arrival at Port-aux-Basques after the ninety-six mile trip across Cabot Strait. Some expressed a premonition of danger and lay on their berths without undressing. Others stayed up late playing cards in the saloon. A few safety-minded men made trips to their assigned life-boat stations so as to be familiar with the route. On the bridge Capt. Ben Tavnor talked with the purser, Tom Fleming. The Captain thought it would have been safer if their escort, the minesweeper *HMCS Grandmere*, sailed along in front of them rather than astern, but these were orders from the Navy. He was also told to sail in a zig-zag pattern to avoid possible torpedoes. Looking out over the ocean, Tom Fleming mentioned what a lovely calm night it was. "Calm, alright," said Tavnor, "but not lovely for us. The smoke is going straight up in the sky and can be seen for miles on a night like this." He was right. Five miles away, a German sub had just surfaced to charge batteries. It was 3:00 a.m. and they were only 40 miles from their destination.

The log of the U-69, made public after the war, read, *"Oct. 14, 0300 hours NDT Sighted freighter followed by warship. We are preparing to attack."*

In the bright moonlight the *Caribou* was an easy target and at 3:30 a.m. a torpedo hit the starboard side with devastating results. Many passengers died instantly. The ship's boilers blew up, killing everyone in the engine room. The lights went out and there was panic below deck as people tried to find their way up in the darkness. Many could not remember their lifeboat station number and those who went to the starboard side found their lifeboats blown to bits by the torpedo. On the port side two lifeboats that were already hanging out over the side were lowered into the water by the crew. As passengers jumped in, the boats began filling with water. There were holes in the bottom to drain rainwater and someone had

The *S.S. Caribou* was carrying troops and civilians when she was torpedoed by a German U-boat on Oct. 14, 1941. 101 persons survived but 137 died in the tragedy. A 1-10 Courtesy of "The Rooms" Provincial Archives Division

neglected to put back the plugs. In the first boat the plugs were found and replaced and that boat got away safely but the second one began sinking and overturned, throwing the unfortunate occupants into the cold water. At the stern of the *Caribou* the remaining two lifeboats were still on deck attached to the davits, but before they could be swung out over the side, they were filled with people. There was no way the crew could handle the boats now and they implored the passengers to get out so they could pull the boats from the deck and lower them into the water. The frightened people refused to move. The ship was sinking fast and when it went under it pulled the two lifeboats with it as they were still attached to the davits. Purser Tom Fleming had helped many passengers aboard the first lifeboats in the five minutes the *Caribou* remained afloat and was trying to free a life raft when he felt the deck go under. Realizing people are often sucked to their deaths when a ship sinks, he took a deep breath and went down with the ship. But not far. Tom was a strong swimmer and was determined not to die now. With lungs almost bursting he came to the surface, helped in no small way by the lifejacket he was wearing. All around people were clinging to life rafts, pieces of wreckage, and the one lifeboat that managed to stay afloat. Some were crying, others were dying. Still others were shouting the names of loved ones, hoping to hear the reply "I'm here!" Some did. Fleming was the only ship's officer to survive. All the others including Capt. Ben Tavnor and his two sons, Harold and Stanley, were lost.

On board the *Grandmere* the crew heard the explosions and sighted the sub on the surface. The bridge ordered "Full speed ahead," and steered straight for the U-boat, hoping to ram it. The sub crash-dived and barely avoided a collision. The minesweeper immediately dropped a pattern of depth charges but saw no evidence of damage to a submarine. *Grandmere's* Captain, Lieutenant James Culbert, knew there had to be survivors in the water but was required to follow standing orders and these were basically 'Keep chasing the sub and don't worry about survivors.' The reasoning seems to be that if the minesweeper stopped to pick up survivors, then it too would probably be torpedoed.

After a frustrating and fruitless search, the *Grandmere* returned to the scene of the sinking and as the sun rose at 7:30 a.m., one hundred and three survivors were taken from the water One man who was saved was R.C.M.P. Corporal W.B Rouse, who was returning to Newfoundland to be married. Strangely enough, although the ill-fated ship was headed for Newfoundland, all the survivors were brought back to Nova Scotia. Two men died before they reached land. Later that day many fishermen from the Port-aux-Basques area went out in their long liners and recovered several bodies.

Dr. Paul O'Neill, already mentioned earlier, told me that his mother, my aunt Jo, and another lady were the only women on the previous trip of the Caribou and as far as she knew, all the other passengers were military men.

The *Garland* Disaster

Although this tragedy was not war-related, it did occur during the war and I recall the terrible loss of twenty-two lives when two Bell Island ferries collided and sank in Conception Bay. The date was Nov. 10, 1940.

Hundreds of miners who lived around the bay were returning to the island having spent the weekend at home, and that Sunday afternoon was a busy one on the Tickle, the three-mile route from Portugal Cove to the island. The ferry *W. Garland*, in the charge of Capt. Abbott and engineer Norman Ash, left the cove at 5:30 with 24 passengers on board. It should never have been allowed to leave the pier. It had no license to carry passengers, had no lifebelts, and the one lifeboat that came with the ship when purchased was left ashore to make room for more freight. Also, incredibly, the red and green port and starboard running lights had burned out and were never replaced.

At Bell Island, the other ferry, the *Little Golden Dawn*, had just discharged a load of passengers and started its return trip to the cove for more miners at 5:40 with only Capt. Mitchell and engineer Dos Rose on board. That ferry had a serious mechanical defect as well, and when Capt. Mitchell saw the white lights of the *Garland* straight ahead in the darkness, he attempted to sound a warning with the ship's horn, but it would not work. My father once told me one of the 'Rules of the Road' at sea when approaching another vessel in darkness was "Red to Red; Green to Green." In other words, if you see a red light ahead, you steer your ship to the right so that your red light faces that red light. Do the same thing with green and the vessels would pass each other safely. Also, he said, if no running lights are seen, then you keep to the right. Whether or not the *Golden Dawn* had running lights is not known, but the *Garland* correctly turned to starboard or right. Unfortunately the *Golden Dawn* made a wrong turn and sailed directly into the path of the *Garland*. The latter was an old wooden ship and much of the timber was rotten; when it crashed into the side of the *Golden Dawn*, the front of the ship disintegrated and it sank in less than five minutes, leaving 26 people struggling in the cold water. The engineer of the *Golden Dawn* had stopped the engine after the crash and was unable to start it. That ship had no lifeboat either and it drifted away from the helpless people clinging to wreckage in the water. It was also leaking badly from a hole in the side and the two men on board worked feverishly with hand pumps trying to keep it afloat. The accident happened only a few hundred yards from the island.

The owner of the *Golden Dawn*, Fred Snow, was standing on the pier and heard cries for help. He immediately set out in a motor boat with Walter Dicks and another man as the Home Defense Unit switched on a powerful searchlight. Four people were pulled from the water: the engineer Ash, a Mr. Tucker, and a Mr. Quilty and his cousin. Two other passengers were also taken from the water but they passed away before being taken ashore. Capt. Abbott and twenty-one passengers died on that cold November afternoon.

Another motor boat went to the scene and towed the *Golden Dawn* back to the island where it quickly sank with no one on board.

Other Wartime Memories

The Commission of Government ordered a complete blackout for St. John's and all points east of Holyrood in April, 1942. Householders were ordered to cover all windows with shutters, dark blinds, or blackout material and remove bulbs from their porch lights. All motor vehicles were required to have shields on their headlights so that no light was visible from above. Drivers could then see the road only a few yards ahead and thus had to drive very slowly at night. As well, cars had to have four-inch wide bands of white paint on all fenders. Sometimes in summer my older brother took us trouting on the Salmonier Line, where we fished till dark. While driving back home he used the full headlights until we reached Holyrood. Then he put the shields in place and literally crawled back to town. This happened only a couple of times and after that he made sure we got back home before dark.

In town, storekeepers not only were required to have their windows covered, they had to have a dark curtain inside the doors so that when opened, no light was visible from the outside. There was some difficulty walking the streets at nighttime when there was no moon. People kept walking into telephone poles. It turned out to be a great explanation when some guys got into a fight downtown and came home with a black eye. "I walked into a telephone pole." It got so bad the government ordered utility companies to paint white stripes around the wooden poles. The blackout was strictly enforced and a volunteer group of air raid wardens monitored the situation. These men, many of them turned down for military service because of age or other reasons, were issued stirrup pumps and buckets of sand to help douse fires in case of an incendiary bomb attack. Air raid sirens were located on towers in various locations in the city, although we had no air raid shelters. Nevertheless every few days or nights the wailing of a practice alert was heard and residents would say "Peter is at it again." Peter Cashin, the renowned politician, was head of the Home Defense organization. The blackout regulations were relaxed somewhat in August 1943, and street lighting, prohibited entirely during the blackout, was permitted at half the brightness of pre-war conditions. The Light and Power Company found that in the previous fourteen months 150 street lights had been destroyed by vandals.

Car drivers had other problems not related to the blackout. Tires were rationed. Taxis and other commercial vehicles owners could buy new tires but owners of private cars were not permitted to buy them and it was a common sight to see a driver stopped along the side of a road fixing a flat tire. Some men even bought old cars just to get the tires. Tea and sugar were rationed with only a limited amount being allowed for each family member, including children. Ration coupons were issued by the government and had to be surrendered to grocery stores upon the purchase of these products. I remember not liking strong tea and trading my coupons with my siblings for their sugar coupons.

A familiar sight in St. John's during the war years when new tires were unobtainable for private cars. Here, Neil Kennedy and Walter Simms fix a flat tire. Note white "War Paint" on car fender.
Photo by Frank Kennedy

All outgoing mail was opened at the post offices and censored. Any reference to military personnel was deleted, even if it was such a seemingly harmless remark such as "It's nice to have my brother John home on leave." The slogan was "Loose lips sink ships." All photofinishers were instructed to destroy any photos showing coastline or shipping of any kind. The photo of the *Edmund B. Alexander* accompanying this chapter would have been destroyed had I taken the film to a regular photofinisher, but being an amateur photographer at the time, I developed it myself.

St. John's, being the most easterly port in North America, was often the starting point for trans-Atlantic convoys and many merchant ships from the mainland stopped here to await naval escort to Britain. Many warships lay at anchor in the harbour waiting for what was considered a full complement of ships for a convoy. Consequently sometimes there were thousands of sailors roaming the streets. A Canadian government official who visited the city claimed in a report that there were 8,000 Canadian sailors in port and they were responsible for excessive drunkenness and brawling in downtown St. John's. He went on to say the sailors smashed so many store windows that the store owners had the windows boarded up. That man must have been downtown only at night and didn't realize that the windows were boarded up because of the blackout regulations, not because they were being broken. Local police were kept busy regardless and were helped out by the Canadian Naval Shore Patrol who also patrolled the city. The U.S. soldiers from Fort Pepperell and later U.S. Airmen were not entirely innocent and they had police patrols in place as well.

Security was beefed up considerably after the disastrous fire at the K. of C. Hostel on Dec. 12, 1942, which killed 99 people, many of them servicemen. That tragedy was described in detail in a previous book, *Flashes From the Past*, and I will not go into it here except to say that an inquiry found the fire was definitely arson, possibly by an enemy agent. Evidence was also discovered at the Red Triangle Club that preparations had been made to torch that building as well. The telephone exchange building on Duckworth Street and the Light and Power substation on the South Side were put under 24-hour-guard for fear of sabotage, as was the power station at Petty Harbour.

End of the War

World War II came to a close on May 8, 1942, when Germany surrendered to the Allies, but not before nine hundred Newfoundlanders had paid the supreme sacrifice. These brave men gave their lives so that we who are left behind may see peace in our day. Their names will be forever remembered.

Many Newfoundlanders stationed in England during the war courted and married English ladies and brought them back to Newfoundland when the war ended. Stories are told of how some of the men enticed their brides back to this land of milk and honey. Some blushing brides were in for a letdown. A sailor from the Northern Peninsula had just returned to the island with his bride, and they were standing at a streetcar stop on Water Street near the Red Triangle Club. After waiting nearly ten minutes the lady was overheard remarking to the 'tar' in a fine British accent "Well, I hope the streetcar service is better than this in Flower's Cove."

chapter 16

BEFORE
I FORGET

Santa Claus came twice

Not all the kids in our neighborhood had this fringe benefit of belief in Santa Claus. At our house he came twice. The usual visit, of course, was on Christmas Eve but we were told that on Old Christmas Day, Santa made another run around with a few things he had left over from Christmas. We hung up our stockings on January 6, and sure enough, to our delight, next morning we found some candy and other goodies and an apple or orange. Great! Being the youngest of six children, I was the last member of the family to believe in Santa. I mean, let's face it, my mother said there was a real Santa Claus and she would never lie. After all these years I still remember one morning having breakfast in our kitchen and my mother left the room to go upstairs and "make the beds". In less than a minute she was back and told me excitedly "I just saw Santa Claus out in the hall!" I jumped up and ran out to the hall but saw no one. I shouted "He's not there now, mom." She said sympathetically "Oh that's too bad, my son. He must have just left."

I recall too, the sad day I found out the truth. Santa Claus brought goodies only to those who believed in him, and finally none of my siblings bothered hanging up their stockings anymore. That year with so many of my young peers scoffing at me for my childishness, I decided to find out for myself. On that particular Christmas Eve, after my mother and the older children had gone to Midnight Mass, I sneaked down to our dining room where my mother kept a large bowl of fruit in a cupboard. I carefully counted the apples and oranges and went back to bed. In those days we hung up our stockings at the foot of our bed, supposedly so that Santa would know who's who. On Christmas morning I awoke early and was very pleased to find the set of trains I had requested earlier, and my stocking stuffed with candy, nuts and other goodies and an apple and an orange. Rushing down to the dining room I knelt down and opened the cupboard door and again counted the apples and oranges. I counted them twice. One of each was missing. I can still picture in my mind, this poor little boy kneeling beside that open cupboard door, staring at the bowl of fruit and sitting back on his heels in disbelief, confusion, and finally the realization that this was it. This wonderful childhood dream was wiped out. Forever! I went slowly back to my bedroom and half-heartedly played with my new trains. I didn't tell my mother of my discovery for many weeks. I didn't want her to be also disappointed that Christmas. But I kept thinking, I suppose the next thing I'll find out is that there's no Tooth Fairy either.

Save the Wrappers

Purity Molasses Kisses were a popular confection in the 1930s and still are to this day. They cost one cent for two and came in several flavors. As a promotional stunt, every Saturday morning Purity factories paid ten cents for every 100 wrappers brought in. Several friends saved these wrappers for me and when I had one hundred I went to the Purity factories office on Hamilton Street and lined up with dozens of the other children waiting for their wrappers to be counted and to be paid the dime per hundred. Counting the wrappers was a time-consuming job for the Purity office employee, but for us it was worth the wait because we left that office with the price of a movie that afternoon.

The 'Funny Papers'

Question—What was the maiden name of Dagwood Bumstead's wife, Blondie? Answer later. In the mid-'30s my friend Art Kane and I went every Saturday to a wholesale book and newspaper store on New Gower Street and bought comics at reduced rates. This was some years after Purity factories discontinued buying candy wrappers. The comics or "funny papers" as they were called, were published weekly, and if all copies were not sold, the wholesaler could get a refund by providing proof of the unsold copies. Instead of sending all the papers back he simply cut off the names and sent these back for a full refund. Then he sold the nameless papers at half price and Art and I took advantage of the bargain. There was a variety of comics and we each bought different issues and after reading them traded with each other.

There was a great assortment of characters in the "funnies." Some of the more memorable included Major Hoople (*Our Boarding House*), Maggie and Jiggs (*Bringing Up Father*), Tarzan, Popeye the Sailor, Mutt and Jeff, Dick Tracy, Out Our Way and The Captain and the Kids. Most of these are long gone but Blondie and Dagwood just go on forever, although its creator, Chic Young, died several years ago. Today Blondie is arguably the favorite comic strip in St. John's and in Newfoundland. It was, without a doubt, the most popular comic strip in the United States for more that 25 years and is seen all over the world in seventeen languages. Blondie first appeared in print in 1930 and has been going strong for over 75 years. Dagwood Bumstead was the son of a millionaire and fell in love with Blondie Boopadoop. He wanted to marry her but his father warned him that if he married this "gold-digging flapper," he would be disinherited. They married in 1933 regardless, and true to his word, that was the last we saw of Dagwood's upper-crust parents, and Dagwood had to get a job for the first time in his life. He went to work with Mr. Dithers and has been with him ever since. In 1935 Dagwood had his first collision with the postman while rushing out the front door, late for work. Surprisingly, that postman has survived many violent crashes but thankfully never did retire. We'd miss him. In 1936 the Woodleys moved in next door and have been good neighbors ever since, although not without the occasional spat over borrowed tools, That year too, Dagwood began making his famous outrageous sandwiches and the pet dog, Daisy, showed up; by now she must be hundreds of years old in dog years. Two children came along, Alexander and Cookie, and actually grew up in the comics over the years. Fortunately for us, and thanks to Chic Young's son, Dean, the Bumsteads never grew old and hopefully will continue bringing weekly smiles to our faces for years to come.

First Animated Neon Sign

In 1925 The Newfoundland Butter Company opened a factory on LeMarchant Road just west of Campbell Avenue. The name was a misnomer, however, as they never did make butter, but Green Label and Solo margarine. Everyone called it "butter" just the same and it really looked like butter. The company also produced pasteurized milk. When Newfoundland joined Canada in 1949, we were the only province permitted by law to make yellow margarine. The other provinces were allowed to make only the white product but since Newfoundland had been using yellow margarine for nearly 25 years, it was written in to the terms of union that the practice could continue.

On the roof of the one story building in the early '30s a huge billboard, in the shape of a cow, but much larger than life, was installed. It was outlined in bright red neon. At night the cow's head nodded up and down and the tail wagged back and forth. The sign was a great attraction for many years but with the coming of war and the blackout, it was prohibited, and after a few years, this outstanding one-of-a-kind symbol was dismantled.

Early Radio

In the early '30s my brother, Eugene, built a crystal set radio and it actually worked. There was no speaker, only a pair of earphones, and no visible power supply, but it worked just the same. I remember he had a coil of fine wire on a cardboard tube, about three inches in diameter and six inches long. It was a discarded VIM can, and the crystal was a tiny lump of shiny metal not much larger than a split pea, mounted in a small container of lead. In order to receive a broadcast, Eugene's friend, Howard Dicks, told him, he needed a ground wire and an antennae. The ground was easy. It was just a wire connected to a water pipe, but the antennae should be on the roof, so Eugene and Howard climbed our ladder with a large coil of copper wire and surveyed the situation. They decided to tie one end of the wire to a chimney pot of the adjoining Pike home and stretch it across our roof to one of our chimneys. Having fastened one end to the Pikes' chimney, they walked across the roof and began securing the other end. The wire sagged considerably and Howard told Eugene to pull it tight. He did so and there was a resounding crash as the large earthenware chimney pot tumbled to the roof and smashed into pieces. Undaunted, they tied the wire around the chimney and let it go at that. Mrs. Pike came rushing out to see what had caused the noise and spotted the two young men on the roof. My mother appeared as well, and when she found out what had happened, assured Mrs. Pike that she would pay for the damage. Eugene was warned never to go on that roof again and he didn't need to, as he had strung the wire down over the side of the house and in through the dining room window and it worked very well. Radio stations VOCM and VONF were not yet on the air but Eugene received sporadic transmissions from some mainland and American stations, The best reception came from the Methodist Wesley radio station, just two blocks from our home.

When that station first came on the air in 1924, the spirit of ecumenism was already flourishing in Newfoundland. Well, certainly in St. John's. Well, certainly in the West End. Well, certainly on Patrick Street! The station needed two expensive one-hundred-foot masts for an antennae and one was supplied by an Anglican businessman and the other by a prominent Roman Catholic. Wesley's minister, Dr. J.G. Joyce, a man of great vision, was responsible for setting up this pioneer radio station, the first in Newfoundland and the only church-run radio station in North America. The broadcasting studio and transmitter were located in the church building on Patrick Street, just two miles west of the site where Marconi received the first trans-Atlantic wireless signal twenty-three years earlier. Dr. Joyce reasoned it would be an advantage for people unable to attend church services to be able to hear them on radio. This was his original intention and his motto "We Serve," still follows through more than eighty years later. The church is now affiliated with the United Church of Canada.

When Dr. Joyce sought donations to cover the cost if equipment, he met with a certain amount of opposition. Some members of his congregation declared, "This newfangled contraption is the Devil's own work." Nevertheless, by the end of June, 1924, one thousand dollars had been raised and the station went on the air in July. He was determined to have no commercial advertising and hoped to have volunteers run the station. His dream was fulfilled and what started out as a 100 watt transmitter with call letters 8WMC steadily progressed over the years to to-day's 10,000 watt VOWR (voice of Wesley Radio) now operating 24 hours a day and bringing programs of all faiths and a great variety of music to the airwaves. The powerful transmitter is now located on Mount Scio Road. The station continues to be run by a group of dedicated volunteers and is financed by public donations, plus substantial revenue from an annual radio auction.

Now to return to Eugene's tale. He purchased a battery radio in the late '30s, and by now had several other choices for his listening pleasure. VOCM had come on the air in 1936 and the government station, VONF, later to become CBC, commenced broadcasting in 1939. In the 1940s, another station could be heard daily during regular business hours. It was VOAS, the Voice of Ayre and Sons and originated from the music department of that firm's three-story department store on Water Street. They played their own records, interspersed with commercials, plugging products for sale in their various departments. At that time, before the coming of CDs, cassettes, long play records or 45s, the only source of music available for replay was the old 78 rpm platters, and the maximum length on one side was only three minutes. If you wished to buy a record you could take it into a private booth and play it yourself before making the purchase. If you didn't like it, no sale. No harm done.

As mentioned, Eugene's new radio was a battery set .There were two "dry" batteries and a big 6-volt car battery. The 6-volt battery had to be charged every three or four weeks and I remember that winter Eugene borrowed my wooden slide and took the battery down to The Royal Garage on Carnell Street for that purpose. Next day he picked up the battery and hauled it back on my slide. This radio, an Atwater-Kent, had a large speaker and we enjoyed the novelty of hearing programs from many countries. Eugene's favorite foreign station, at least for best reception, seemed to be KDKA in Schenectady, New York.

With the opening of Fort Pepperell in 1941, another radio station appeared on the air waves and was a favorite with many city residents. It was VOUS, the Voice Of United States. That station was commercial free and had basically all American programming including most of the top radio shows of the era. With the closing down of Pepperell, that station went off the air. As well as CBC, VOCM, and VOWR, today we have VOAR, run by the Seventh Day Adventist Church and CHMR, MUN radio, run by the students of Memorial University.

St. John's, Never a One-Horse Town

When I was growing up in St. John's, horses were a common sight. Hundreds trotted around the streets daily, hauling anything from a half-ton of coal to a wagon load of fresh bread. Most business firms had several long carts. These were simple long wooden frames with two wheels and were used mainly for carrying barrels and cases of goods. Most homes in the city were heated with coal stoves and coal furnaces and the coal was delivered in box cars, which were, as the name suggests, a square open-top wooden box with two wheels. Grocery stores, like A. V. Duffy's, used four wheel wagons with a seat for the driver. In winter all converted to sleighs and even the few taxi cabs in the city were put away in favor of one-horse open sleighs. These taxi-sleighs had one long padded seat running the length of the sleigh with a padded back, so that the passengers rode side-on to the direction of travel, and the driver sat on a small seat at the rear. A large blanket was always provided for the comfort of the passengers and the tinkle of the sleigh bells added to the enjoyment of the ride. The Newfoundland Constabulary used horses for decades until 1951, when they switched to patrol cars. One local wit proclaimed "They stopped riding horses and started riding clutches." The Royal Newfoundland Constabulary began using horses again in 2003 when two of the four-legged creatures joined the force. They have been used for show on some state occasions and have been used effectively for crowd control. A horse parade was held annually for a number of years and we really enjoyed watching that. I note that in 1939, one hundred and fifty animals took part, all pulling decorated carriages, long carts and various types of wagons. It was a busy afternoon for the street cleaners. In winter, horse races were held on Quidi Vidi lake and were very popular. In 1994 however, a pickup truck that was parked out on the pond went through the ice and the driver nearly drowned. That was the last year the horse races were held on the lake.

The Eight O'Clock Whistles

Many factories in the city had machinery operated by steam power, and on their roofs a whistle similar to a locomotive whistle which was blown at the start of work at 8:00 a.m.. Those I remember were Purity Factories on Hamilton Street; Harvey-Brehm, Water Street East; Nfld. Boot and Shoe, Job Street; Nfld. Boot and Shoe, Sudbury Street; The Rope Walk (Colonial Cordage), Mundy Pond; Horwood Lumber Co., Water Street; Nfld. Nail and Foundry, Hamilton Street; and Imperial Tobacco Co., Flavin Street. The shrill whistles could be heard all over the city and sounded within a few seconds of each other, depending on the accuracy of the whistle blower's watch. Most businesses sounded the whistles at five to eight, as well as on the hour. For us it was the signal to get out of bed and get ready for school. It took us only four minutes to run down to Holy Cross and we always ran. When a whistle awoke us we would shout, "Is that the first whistle?" If someone answered, "Yes," that would give us another glorious five minutes for a little snooze.

With the change from steam to electric power the whistles were gradually phased out. Unfortunately, so were most of the factories. The only survivor from the above group seems to be the Purity Factories, which many years ago moved to a new, larger plant on Blackmarsh Road as their business continued to flourish.

The Four Seasons

Signs of Spring

Playing marbles on the sidewalk. As soon as the snow had melted and the gravel sidewalks dried up, here we were with our heels pressed into the ground, spinning around making a hole we called "a mot." The marbles were tiny shiny earthenware balls a half-inch in diameter, in various colors. Glass alleys were also used. They came in different sizes from a half- to one-inch, the latter being 'worth' ten marbles. Hop-scotch was another popular spring game where a series of connected squares were drawn on the street and had to be hopped into and out of on one foot. If a player stepped on a line he was out. Rolling a hoop was great fun too. Where we got them, I don't know, but we raced up and down Patrick Street driving our metal hoops with a stick, pretending we were driving a car.

Signs of Summer

In warm weather we walked in to Mundy Pond and went swimming in the pond behind the present Purity Factories on Blackmarsh Road. Having already put on our bathing trunks at home under our slacks, we needed no change house to undress and there was none, but after a good swim we ran around and played until the trunks dried. Bowring Park was another popular area for swimming. There was no pool at Bannerman Park at that time but the 'east-enders' used the natural pool in Rennies' River.

There was good trouting back then within walking distance of the city. A favorite spot was "The Captains," a pool on South Brook just above Bowring Park. That would be a full day trip, usually finished off with a boil-up and a nice cup of tea with some potted meat sandwiches, which our mother had prepared for us. On other occasions Mike O'Brien and I walked up to George's Pond on Signal Hill and caught pricklies. I don't mean small trout, but tiny fish two inches long, much smaller than sardines, with a thorn protruding from their sides. They weren't very smart and we often caught then by scooping them out of the water with our hands. Sometimes we brought them home alive in bottles, but by the next day they had usually died. Then, of course, there had to be a funeral. The coffin was a match box and the hearse was a tiny toy wagon. The small funeral procession wended its way the full length of our backyard to the already prepared grave site and there the interment was successfully completed with a sucker stick used as a grave marker.

The favorite summer drink was lemon crystal made by dissolving the crystals in water and adding sugar. The actual dry crystals, about the size of the head of a match, were manufactured in England and came in small bottles. I still enjoyed this refreshing drink when I grew up and it became harder to find in stores. I wrote the company, having found their address on a bottle, and asked if they could name a supplier in Newfoundland. They answered they were very sorry but because of the large selection of ready-made soft drinks, sales of lemon crystals dropped off and they had had to discontinue its manufacture. After I went on the staff of the CBC, sometimes when we were on assignment in outports I visited small shops and was able to buy up their few remaining bottles of my favorite beverage.

Signs of Autumn

In late September we went again to Mundy Pond and picked blueberries, which were very plentiful in the same location where we had been swimming earlier. Southside Hill was another good blueberry area. We walked down Patrick Street, across the railway trestle and went straight up the hill. The side facing the city was blue with berries and you could sit down and pick them in perfect comfort. "Cowboys and Indians" was a great game in the fall. It required a lot of running around which was okay in the cool weather. For some unknown reason the Indians were always the bad guys. Thinking back, I suppose it was because they were always shown to be the bad guys in the movies. It took a lot of persuasion to have some of us play that part but it was great fun. Some of us had cap guns, others used a piece of wood shaped like a gun and we ran along the street at full speed, slapping ourselves on our hip and shouting "Bang! Bang! You're dead!", imagining we were on horseback. Another game was "Hide and Seek," where one boy was required to cover his eyes and count to fifty while all the other players scooted to various hiding places. Sometimes the admonishment "No peeking!" could be heard as the counter attempted to see where some boys were hiding. After the count of fifty, the shout "I'm coming!" was heard and the search began. Last one found was the counter for the next game. Sometimes a guy would get tired of the game and instead of hiding went home and was never found.

Signs of Winter

With the first gentle snowfall we could be seen walking around the streets, heads up, tongues out, catching the snowflakes. With the first few inches of snow, on went the mitts and out came the slides and away we went. Long narrow patches of ice appeared on the sidewalks here and there and it was fun running along and skating on these with just our overshoes until some safety-minded residents, seeing the danger, scattered ashes over the slippery spots and ended our fun. There was a lot more fun, though, for as more snow fell and cars disappeared from the streets, we built snow forts and had snowball battles. When the snow was damp, we rolled big 'bumpers' and made snow men with a couple of pieces of coal for the eyes and a small carrot for the nose. Contests developed to see who could make the best snowman.

Rest in Peace

I remember wakes and funerals that took place when I was growing up in St. John's. They were a lot different than today. Women never attended funerals; only men did. The men walked behind a horse-drawn hearse, preceded by the funeral director in his top hat and formal attire. I recall the city's mayor, Andy Carnell, walking in front of the hearse at many funerals, not because he was mayor, but because he was owner of Carnells' Carriage Factory and Funeral Home, located at the corner of Duckworth and Cochrane Streets. There were no funeral homes, per se, and all the wakes took place in the homes of the deceased, usually in the front room or parlor. The wakes went on all day and all night non-stop, for at least two nights and two days. The big crowd came after supper and while the ladies sat around in the parlor with the deceased, the men sat in the kitchen, sometimes playing cards. This was not considered disrespectful and no offence was ever taken. Often a boiled dinner was served and a party atmosphere prevailed throughout the night.

Most of the coffins were made right here in St. John's and some were even made to order. It was reported that one, not-so-gracious undertaker, when called to a home where someone had passed away, would remark, "I'm sorry for your trouble. What's the size of 'im?" The actual funeral started from the home of the deceased and slowly proceeded through the streets directly to the cemetery. Sometimes a stop was made at a church for a short service. If the interment was to be in Belvedere cemetery, a service was held in a chapel right there on the grounds. Unfortunately this chapel was destroyed by fire and never rebuilt. As already mentioned, women and children would never attend funerals but went separately to the church and cemetery to say a final farewell to their loved ones.

chapter 17

THINGS YOU
NEVER
SEE ANYMORE

Whitewash Prices on Shop Windows

A common sight in the '20s and '30s before supermarkets came to St. John's. Some clever storekeepers retraced the printing on the inside of the glass so that if rain or vandals erased the outside words, the message remained. The last store I remember using this method of advertising was Williams' Grocery, at the corners of Patrick St. and Hamilton Ave., who were still using it just a few years ago.

Cars with Skid Chains

Before snow tires became available, most cars in St. John's were put away for the winter but some brave souls used skid chains, which turned out to be noisy and sometimes slipped off the tires and left the car stuck in the snow. Here Bill Taylor and Pat Yard prepare for hunting on the Witless Bay line.
Photo by Rafe O'Neill

Box Cameras

This 3"x5" Model A Brownie was made by Eastman Kodak Co. in Rochester, New York and patented Oct. 6, 1914, and is still in good working order. Unfortunately the film, size 130, is no longer available. Specs. for photo buffs: One shutter speed, 1/25 sec. Two f stops, about f22 and f11. Focal length 4 inches.

A train stuck in snow in Witless Bay

This shot was taken with the Brownie box camera in1927.
Photo by Rafe O'Neill

The view from the Basilica grounds

A favorite tourist attraction, this view was shut out by a block of houses with permission of City Council.
Photo by Frank Kennedy

Now We See

A black fence and a row of black houses.
Photo by Frank Kennedy

Children playing on Shamrock Field

Adults also used the grounds extensively for soccer and other sports. Every summer bus loads of handicapped children spent a day enjoying various sporting activities on the wide open space.
Photo by Frank Kennedy

Now We See

A large parking lot and a supermarket which was built inspite of strong protests from neighborhood residents.
Photo by Frank Kennedy

A moose on Shamrock Field

This fellow wandered into the field a few years ago and a city bus driver stopped to let passengers see the unusual sight. The animal was escorted back into the woods by the Wildlife people and as mentioned, Shamrock Field has also disappeared.
Photo by Frank Kennedy

Drunks lying near the Liquor Store

Since liquor was not allowed to be consumed on the premises, it's a mystery how this guy got there.
Photo by Frank Kennedy

Rennie's River Swimming Pool

This pool opened in 1928 and was very popular. By the late fifties Rennie's River became polluted and the pool was closed down. A few years later a pool was built in Bannerman Park and is still in operation. Many indoor pools in the city are now in operation all year round.
Photo by Frank Kennedy

A Horse trough in St. John's

This one is in Bowring Park and was the last one of several located in the downtown. It stood for many years at the top of Prescott Street near Rawlin's Cross. Note the small troughs for thirsty dogs.
Photo by Frank Kennedy

Horses and Sleds in St. John's

On Cavendish Square horses refresh themselves as the drivers have a gab early in the twentieth century. In the background we are looking west on Military Road.

Radio Licence Notices

Form 1253 Dicks
DEPARTMENT OF POSTS AND TELEGRAPHS
RADIO LICENCE NOTICE

Dear Sir or Madam:

I have to bring to your notice that —— a —— Radio Licence for the
your
operation of a Wireless Receiving Set —— expired on the 31st December
——————————————— has not been paid

Continued operation without a Licence constitutes a breach of the
Radio Telegraph Act of 1930, and amendments thereto.

I shall be glad, therefore, if you will kindly arrange to
obtain
——————— your Licence for the year 194   as soon after receipt of
renew
this notice as possible. Licences may be obtained from any Post
Office or in outlying districts from members of the Ranger Force.

Yours faithfully,

Secretary.

In 1930 the Responsible Government brought in The Radio Telegraph Act requiring every home with a radio to have a radio licence. It had to be renewed every year and if not, the above notice would be sent out. The act was thought to be a good source of revenue, but the cost of enforcement outweighed the returns and after a few years, the idea was scrapped.

Liquor Permits

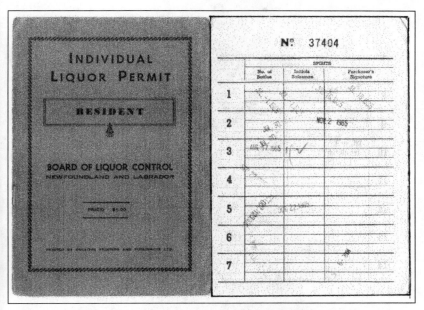

For several years liquor could not be purchased in Newfoundland without a permit, and then only three bottles a week were allowed. The permit was stamped with each purchase. The system was a great boost for the bootleg business. It was quite easy to buy a permit and they cost only one dollar. Many bootleggers visited graveyards and copied down names from the headstones and took out permits in the names of the dead. No I.D.s were ever required. On the other hand if one was having a wedding or some such party, one just had to mention that at the liquor store and there was no limit on the amount of booze that could be bought. Needless to say, a large number of "planned weddings" never took place.

Fire Alarm Boxes

A common sight in the city in the first half of the 20th century, hundreds of these were connected directly to the fire department and there was absolutely no doubt where the call came from, as the box number was punched into a ticker tape. However, they were phased out with the coming of reliable telephone service.
Photo by Frank Kennedy

A 1937 Eaton's Catalogue

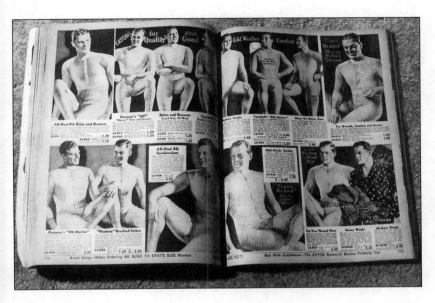

The Prices!

On pages shown:

Men's Drawers ....$1.29 pr.

Fleece lined shirts ....$1.00 ea.

On other pages:

Ladies dresses ....$1.98 ea.

" frocks ....$1.00 up

All wool pullovers...................... .98 ea.

Ladies' slippers.......................... .65 pr.

Men's dress shirts ....$1.00 ea.

" Oxford shoes...............$2.75 pr.

Auto tires, 4 ply ....$6.50 ea.

6 volt car battery......................$5.95 ea.

Baby Brownie camera...............$1.25 ea.

15 Jewel Swiss wrist watch ....$5.00 ea.

The Newfie Bullet

The Newfoundland Railway's *Overland Limited,* was sarcastically named *The Newfie Bullet* by servicemen during World War II. Historian Dr. Paul O'Neill says it is not known whether it originated with U.S. or Canadian troops, but it was due to the slow progress and nearly 200 stops along the 547 miles from Port-aux-Basques to St. John's. A popular joke at the time relates to an upset young lady who told the conductor she was about to give birth. The conductor scolded her for getting aboard the train in that condition, but she replied she was not in that condition when she got on board. The cross-island passenger service began in 1898 before there were any motor cars in Newfoundland and continued for 71 years until 1969. In 1950 the official name was changed to *The Caribou,* but the name *Newfie Bullet* remained as an affectionate title by Newfoundland travelers.

"The End" at the Close of a Movie

It was very nice. The words "The End," appeared, the lights came on and you walked out of the theatre. Now, when a picture ends there seems to be an endless list of credits, from the janitor of the studio to the actor's manicurist. Who cares? Unless you are prepared to sit for another five minutes, you grope your way out of the theatre in the darkness.

"The End" never appears on the last page of a book, either. Except this one.

Photo by Frank Kennedy